Video Production Workshop

Video Production Workshop

Tom Wolsky

Focal Press
Taylor & Francis Group

NEW YORK AND LONDON

Introduction

Who Am I to Write This Book?

I have been teaching video applications for the Digital Media Academy (http://www.digitalmediaacademy.org) for a number of years, primarily at their Stanford University campus, but also at many other locations around the country, and am proud to be on its board of directors. I also taught video production at Mendocino High School, a small, rural high school in northern California, for ten years, before the program was closed due to lack of state funding. I have written a number of books on video editing and well as curriculum for Apple Computer's Video Journalism program. While teaching I have also been a principal of a video production company, South Coast Productions.

Prior to the teaching phase of my life I worked in film and video production for longer than I care to admit. For many years I was at ABC News, as an operations manager and producer, first in London and then in New York. Before joining ABC I was a freelance technician, producer and screenwriter in London after graduating with honors from what was then called the London School of Film Technique, now the London International Film School. My life of many years of continuous education in the ever-changing world of film, video and media production began decades ago at the Communication Arts department at the University of Notre Dame.

Who Is This Book For?

This book is intended for video production students and teachers. Those who are starting out in video production without formal training could also learn a great deal from these pages.

What's on the DVD?

The DVD included with this book contains a few short scenes and some shots that are used to illustrate points made in the book that could perhaps best be illustrated when seen as a sequence or in motion. The disc is divided into a few chapters that correspond to chapters in the book. It would be useful to view the contents of the disc while reading those chapters.

Acknowledgments

First, my special thanks and appreciation to John Giambruno and the students of his video production class at Menlo-Atherton High School, who appear in many of the photographs and on some of the video clips on the DVD; and to Greg Gunkel, for his assitance. As always, my gratitude to all the people at CMP Books who make this book-writing process relatively painless, particularly Paul Temme, associate publisher, for his thoughtful advice and guidance; Dorothy Cox, senior editor, and Gail Saari, for organizing the files I needed and for their great patience and forbearance with me during the final stages of bringing this material together. Many thanks are due to Hastings Hart for so carefully working through the copyediting. Any errors or omissions that remain are the results of my oversights, not his. My thanks to Noel Ekhart for her work on the covers. My thanks as always to Sidney Kramer for his expert advice.

A great many thanks are due to my partner, B. T. Corwin, a superb teacher and photographer without whose skill, endless encouragement, technical support, and patience this book would not have been possible.

Contents

Introduction to Video Production

Many schools have been offering video production for a great many years, going back to the days of closed-circuit television and cameras with vacuum tubes. Editing was usually done clumsily using linear tape decks and copying shots from one machine to another. The advent of low-cost, high-quality digital video in the '90s, together with extraordinarily powerful computers and non-linear editing systems, has made ever-greater numbers of schools take up video production for a variety of reasons. No doubt the afford-ability, compactness, and quality of modern equipment are important factors. Another key factor though is the increasing importance of media, visual and aural, in people's lives. Video and television are now the primary sources of information and entertainment for Americans, particularly young Americans. Because of this it becomes ever more important for today's students to understand how video and television is made and the techniques that can be used to manipulate the medium to produce a response in the audience. If you understand how the medium is created, you can understand how it can impact your life; if you understand how it can manipulate your emotions and responses, you can better control your reactions to the medium. All this combined with the ubiquity of camcorders and digital media in homes has made offering these kinds of programs a logical step in modern education. In today's technology-driven world, the more you understand about various types of technology, the better off you'll be.

Most of today's technology is centered around or connected to the computer, and video production is no different. Everything now is being done digitally. Of course the technologies that drive video production are constantly changing; it seems that no sooner does one format get established than a new and better format is created. The DV format (Figure 1.1), and its variants DVCAM, DVCPRO, and DVCPRO50, are now widely used throughout the world; but HDV (high-definition video) on the same size of tape as DV is available for use in homes and schools (Figure 1.2). Even home editing software is now capable of editing this type of high-definition material. All of this is being controlled by computer software, operating systems, and applications that are constantly changing. This means two things for the teacher using technology, for the instructor of video production in particular, and for their students. One, he or she will have to spend the remainder of their working life in pursuit of more and ever-changing knowledge. Two, it is important that the teacher and his or her students have a firm grasp of the fundamentals of video production—the concepts and best practices of writing, camera work, lighting, sound, and editing that don't change regardless of systems being employed. In the course of this book I will make reference to specific systems and equipment, not so much as a recommendation but more as what is typically employed in schools or in the video industry. This will of course be a constantly moving feast. Last year's hot software will be this year's also-ran. Not that last year's software isn't fully capable; it just may be missing the latest bells and whistles that everyone's talking about. One word of caution about chasing the latest and greatest: they're often not fully developed or tested, and it's often better to wait till the software has been out for while, running on a variety of different operating systems and hardware, before taking the leap into a new product or a new version. This is why the leading edge of technology is often called the bleeding edge of technology.

Figure 1.1 Typical consumer camcorder: Sony TRV9

Figure 1.2 Sony HDV-FX1

Many video production programs have developed out of technology careers and occupations programs in schools, districts, or counties. Film and television production is obviously a major industry in the United States. It is one of the country's largest earners through export. Video production is integrated into practically every corporate entity, government agency, law-enforcement authority, and military department in the country. Video production is fully integrated into most aspects of every business plan, from small businesses creating local advertising and promotional material, through local and regional companies producing informational and training materials, through event and wedding videos, itself a multi-billion dollar industry, all the way to the largest corporations spending a great deal of time, personnel, and resources on public relations, in-house training and presentations, and broadcast advertising.

Types of Production in Schools

There are many reasons schools invest in video production technology. Some of the reasons are beneficial to students, and some have less noble motives. There are many different uses video can be put to, such as the production of school announcements; the taping of school events such as sports; broadcasting school board meetings; a full-scale video journalism course; a video production program that develops creative programming, drama, comedy, music, commercials, documentaries, the traditional fare of film schools; or a program that integrates technology in the core curriculum, using it to engage students in collaborative, team-focused, project-based learning activities. All of these will, to some degree, require different technical skills and a basic understanding of the techniques of video production. Many schools implement some combination of one or more of these types of programs.

Announcements

Announcements are a popular video program production in many schools. They are usually daily live or taped broadcasts, often distributed through closed-circuit television, through a school or even a school district at a regularly scheduled time (Figure 1.3). Often this is a simple announcement read to camera, with the students in the class taking turns, sometimes pairs of students, sometimes individuals. Students working in pairs require more coordination and planning.

Figure 1.3 Student announcements production

These can either be done live to camera and broadcast or transmitted directly, or they can be prerecorded on tape. Either way this is usually done in a small studio specially rigged for this purpose. We'll look at studio facilities in more detail in Chapter 14.

The advantage of this type of a program is that, once the infrastructure is in place, it's easy and quick to put into practice. Within a couple of weeks of the start of the school year you can have a brand new program up and running, producing content and delivering it throughout your system. Students can either take turns presenting on a daily basis, or you can do it for a few days or a week or more. The idea behind you presenting for more than a single day in rotation is that it gives you an opportunity to develop writing, speaking, and presentation skills. Doing it just once means you're less likely to remember how to do it the next time it's your turn. Doing it a few days in a row will make it easier for you to get back into the groove.

Though this type of program is quick to set up, it will take up most, if not all, of a class period even after students have gotten accomplished at the tasks required to get the programming on the air. If at all possible it would be good to supplement this type of program with more activities that will allow students to try a variety of different types of video productions.

Taped Events

Broadening the scope of the announcements program with taped material takes us to another type of production common in schools, taping or broadcasting live events, sports, assemblies, school board meetings, and others (Figure 1.4). This can be done with one or two or more cameras. The output from the cameras can either be taped individually and edited together, which can be time-consuming; or the program can be switched live through a video switcher. This requires more equipment and more personnel to operate and put the program together on the spot. On the other hand, it also affords quick delivery, as the output of the switcher can be recorded to tape and immediately broadcast. A third option, if the facilities are in place, would be to broadcast the live output of the production from the switcher directly to air either on cable or on closed-circuit television.

Live production, as we shall see, is skill-intensive and requires a great deal of equipment, practice, and expertise to execute at a high level. A full live broadcast will require at least a director, a sound mixer, and a camera operator for each camera. A separate technical director to switch the program and a floor manager would be beneficial. In addition to the video switcher and cameras, a great deal of cabling is needed, as well as an audio mixer, microphones, and perhaps most importantly a communications system between the director and everyone else involved in the production. The communications system is usually through headsets with built-in microphones connected to a distribution box by wires or a wireless system through radio transmission. All of this requires substantial expenditure of resources and considerable training to do well and is not the kind of program that can be put into place quickly.

Figure 1.4 Students taping live event

Video Journalism

An extension of taping local events is a full-blown video journalism program (Figure 1.5). This is one of the principal forms of video production programs in schools and one that raises special issues that we will come back to in later chapters.

This type of program entails a great deal of student involvement, commitment, and much work outside the classroom. It is a great way to train students in the technical aspects of video production, as well as giving them many opportunities to practice writing, speaking, and presentation skills. In addition to learning all the technical aspects of video production, issues of journalistic responsibilities and ethics must be considered.

In recent years the profession of journalism, and broadcast journalism in particular, has been greatly diminished by the proliferation of talk radio hosts, shock

Figure 1.5 Student reporter

jocks, and vicious television pundits with personal views and agendas, who call themselves journalists but who are really just media hucksters. A school program should always strive to emulate the best of broadcast journalism, not its worst, and should not be used to produce biased, bigoted, self-serving, or aggressively confrontational programming.

A video journalism program is a great way to get students involved in video production while giving you an opportunity to create important, worthwhile programming that can help the school and your fellow students present an honest and straightforward picture of your school community. Another excellent aspect of a video journalism program is that it lets you learn and practice the technical crafts in a great variety of conditions, indoor and outdoor lighting, with different acoustic situations, and different types of editing from basic narration and picture, to complex edits involving music, dialog, and creative graphics animation.

Video Production

By video production program I mean the type of course commonly given in film schools, one that introduces students to the technical aspects of production as well as giving them the opportunity to work in a variety of formats on different topics. Much of this book is based around this type of production class, beginning with editing and camera instruction and developing skills and expertise in a measured way. It gives students the ability to work in a variety of forms as well as forcing them to focus their skill development on specific areas in sequence.

We start with an editing exercise. It's important to learn the concepts of editing, as this gives you skill and experience not only in the digital technology but also in important concepts about pacing, structure, and how shots interact with each other. Editing shots together is putting together the building blocks of a production. It's the heart of movie-making, story-telling, and information-giving in this medium. If you understand the concepts of editing and what makes a good edit and a good piece, you can then move on to learning how to shoot the right material that can be edited into a good piece of work.

The second step is to learn how to use the camera and to develop skills in camera operation. This will be followed up with a more thorough and detailed exploration of camera techniques and direction.

Before going into larger projects it's important that you have a firm grasp of pre-production requirements and scripting. This can vary from project to project based on the type of project being produced, but there are some fundamentals that apply to every project. Once you have completed a simple project from start to finish, from script to screen, it's then important that you learn more about the skills and techniques of video production, particularly lighting and image control, as well as good audio recording techniques.

At some stage the class might want to consider the option of live recording as in the taped events program. This doesn't have to be only for school activities, but it can also be used for creating original programs, dramas, comedies, and any sort of staged play. It's a technique still commonly used for most sitcoms seen on television. It's also used to integrate different segments of a news program and can be an important part of a video journalism program. Whether you decide to follow this path depends primarily on budget, resources, and available space to create a studio. For a staged production usually more space is required, while for a news program, a school anchor studio can be quite small and could easily be made up within most classrooms.

No part of any serious video production class would be complete without looking at the special effects capabilities of digital video, features such as green screening, motion graphics, animation, compositing and much, much more. Though we will look at some of this, much of it will be beyond the scope of this book and is really best learned from software-specific texts or other resources.

I think it's important to include in every course some way for students to be given the opportunity to produce some special project of their own devising. This allows you the freedom to express yourselves through the medium, and get enthusiastic about what you're creating, giving you a chance to show what you can do and show off what you've learned. This is usually the final project for a course, and makes you go through the whole process of making a video.

The Production Process

Producing a video is a process, often lengthy and time-consuming, that goes through three distinct stages called pre-production, production, and post-production. Each stage requires carefully coordination, execution, and teamwork. Working on video projects almost always means working in teams of various sizes from very small, such as a two-person news crew, to very large as on a feature film or music video production. In professional production not all team members will be involved in every stage on the production, but in school productions it's important that everyone in the team be involved in all the stages of the process. Each member may not contribute to some degree in every stage. Some may be more involved in the production phase, while others may be more involved in the post-production stage.

Pre-Production

The first stage of the process is pre-production, which itself goes through a number of phases. At the beginning of course there is an idea, a story, or a concept. What's this video about? What's the story we're going to tell? Equally important is who this video is for. As you consider what the video is, you have consider who will be viewing your video or who you want to view your video. Who is going to see the video will determine what kind of video you're going to make. If the video is about your school, intended for the student audience, you'd probably make a video that showed the kids at the school, who they are, what they do, the different types of kids, who they interact with, and the different activities they have. If the same concept of a video about your school was intended to be seen by parents or the community, the video might focus on the facilities, the teachers, the courses, and the various extracurricular activities the school offers. The video will succeed to the extent that it is able to determine, target and reach your intended audience.

Videos can be informative or entertaining, but in some way they will have to reach the audience on an emotional level for them to be successful. Whether a production is saddening, enriching, affirming, energizing, amusing, frightening, or thought-provoking, it must have an emotional impact on the audience. The tone and emotional connection between the video and the audience starts in this stage of the process and carries on through all the stages that follow. It begins with the idea and the script.

The more complex the emotion, the more powerfully the video tries to impact the audience, the more difficult it becomes to produce well. Comedy, for instance, is hard to do well; more often than not in student productions the audience laughs at how stupidly the performers are behaving than at anything inherently comedic. Similarly, student productions of horror movies are more often comic than frightening. True pathos is hard to achieve without gifted actors who can convey deep emotions. Thought-provoking or uplifting emotional responses need carefully crafted work, or the production may seem just silly. All of these warnings aside, students should always strive to make the best work possible, to reach for the highest goals they can accomplish. Your first productions might not always be as successful as you might like, but if you are honest with yourselves and the shortcomings of your productions, and you persevere, experience and improved skills and better equipment will see your productions improving by leaps and bounds. There is no special magic to making good videos, just good ideas, good techniques, careful planning, careful execution, and good editing. If you start out with a good idea, you can make a great video. If the idea isn't very good, or the script isn't very good, the video will probably be no better than average. You should always strive for excellence, in every script, in every scene you shoot, in every edit you make. If you do, you'll have a much better chance of producing an excellent video. Nothing less than excellence should be acceptable to you; that should be your mantra and your goal at all times as a film or video maker.

We'll look at the pre-production process in detail in Chapter 6, but in its simple form, it starts with an idea. Once the idea has been found, the concept has to be developed. How are you going to tell the story? The concept then has to be pitched, presented to the executive producer, studio boss, or classroom teacher, that this is a concept worth producing. If the concept is approved a treatment is often written, which is then developed into a script. With the script in hand the production can be planned. A storyboard might be created to help with the visualization of the video. All the myriad details that need to be resolved before production can begin include what locations will be needed, what performers, how many cameras, what kind of audio, how long will it take to do all this, what props are needed, what are the logistics, and how will you get to and from the places you need to be with all the people and equipment involved.

In a large production a series of meetings is usually essential to coordinate all the groups who need to come together to work as a unit, such as scenic and costume designers, camera, lighting, sound, logistics and transportation. In many cases keys scenes will be blocked out and carefully rehearsed for the actors and camera before production starts. Makeup, costume, and lighting tests will be shot. It's better to find out how things will look in the simplicity of the rehearsal room with minimal equipment before you are on location, fiddling to make things work while scores of people, or at least those involved in the production crew, are standing around waiting.

Production

Production is the central stage of the creation of a video. This is the stage at which the performers and technicians are brought together. Here the camera or cameras and microphones are used to commit the script and storyboard to tape, or whatever recording or broadcasting mechanism is being used. The video is usually not shot in the order in which the script is written, but usually in the order that is most cost-effective based on availability of locations, personnel, performers, and equipment. The production stage is often the shortest stage in the process. The scripting and planning on a feature film can take years; while editing and post-production can easily be six months to a year alone for a project that might have taken two or three months to shoot. Though it is the shortest portion of the process, it's obviously the most essential. If the cameras and microphones don't record the images and sound, there is no video. If the performances haven't been captured, there is little that can be done to save the project, short of building everything again with computer-generated images. Some things can be "fixed in post," such as correcting color and enhancing the audio, or re-recording the dialog, but essentially the video story, idea, or concept is captured in the production stage. This essential stage is covered extensively in this book, with chapters on camera, lighting, sound, and studio techniques.

Post-Production

The final stage of the process is post-production. Here the shot material is edited into shape, given its drama, or its documentary thesis structure, having the jumble of videotape arranged into a coherent form. Editing is really the heart of video production, the stage that assembles the pieces. It's so important to the creation process that it is traditionally the first craft that students learn. If you know how the story pieces together, what elements in each scene you need to create the impact you want, you then know how it needs to be shot. If you don't understand the rhythm and timing and pacing of how shots fit together with words and music, it's impossible to shoot material that edits together well. Too many camera operators can take gorgeous pictures of scenery but then ruin them by making moves that are either too fast or too slow, or in the wrong direction so they don't cut well with the rest of the material.

The pacing of the video is determined in the editing, with the editor's sense of rhythm, but if that pacing is not in the material to start with, if shots take too long to develop, or scenes don't get covered sufficiently, the production will suffer and often be ruined.

Post-production will to a large extent be governed by the equipment, particularly the software, you're using. All video editing software does have the same sets of tools to some degree or other, perhaps with different names. Many of today's computer-driven post-production solutions now go far beyond simple editing of digital video material and include ever more sophisticated special effects and animation tools.

Production Personnel

There are many people are involved in the making of a video or film production. These are just some of the many members of the team whose skills and expertise are needed to create a successful production.

Executive Producer

In overall charge is the *executive producer.* In the case of video production in schools in most instances, the classroom teacher is the executive producer in that he or she is ultimately responsible for the content of the finished production and for its suitability and appropriateness to the school audience. Though the classroom teacher has the final responsibility and is the ultimate arbiter as executive producer, as in most productions the real decision making on the content is passed down to the producer.

Producer

The *producer* is responsible for bringing together all the necessary personnel and elements needed to create the production: the writer and the script, the director and his or her vision, the production and post-production personnel who we'll see in a moment. In major productions, the executive producer is usually responsible for gathering the financing necessary to produce the video, while the producer is responsible on a day-to-day basis for how that financing is spent.

Large productions will be managed by a *production accountant* or teams of accountants whose job will be to distribute the money.

There may also be *associate producers* who are usually responsible for making sure everyone knows where they are supposed to be and when. This function may also be the responsibility of *assistant producers* or *unit managers* or sometimes *line producers*, who will deal with it on a day-to-day basis while the movie is being shot. Whoever does it is responsible for making up the call sheet and making sure everyone gets one (Figure 1.6). The call, or shoot sheet, includes all the critical information necessary for the day of shooting, and includes information on who has to be where at what time, the necessary contact information, now usually cell phone numbers. It may even include maps of locations and where facilities like trailers and generators are positioned. On large productions there are often separate call sheets for each department, for makeup, costume, props, lighting, sound, grips, each including a list of what items are needed for that day's coverage.

In addition, there may be a number of *production secretaries* who are responsible for the large amount of record keeping necessary on a big-budget movie.

Writer

Every movie has a script, whether it's a music video, a commercial, a documentary, or narrative fiction; at some point the script is written down. It's the *scriptwriter's* job to get those words down on paper or at least into a word processor. The script may be just a list of what shots go with what lyrics in a song; it may be the sequence and the tagline over a pack shot; it may be a narration written long after the shooting is finished and after the interviews have been done; or it may be an original screenplay or an adaptation of another work. Whatever is involved, even a live sports show, something is written down—the introduction, the points the reporter wants to make, and the talking points the color man wants to bring up in

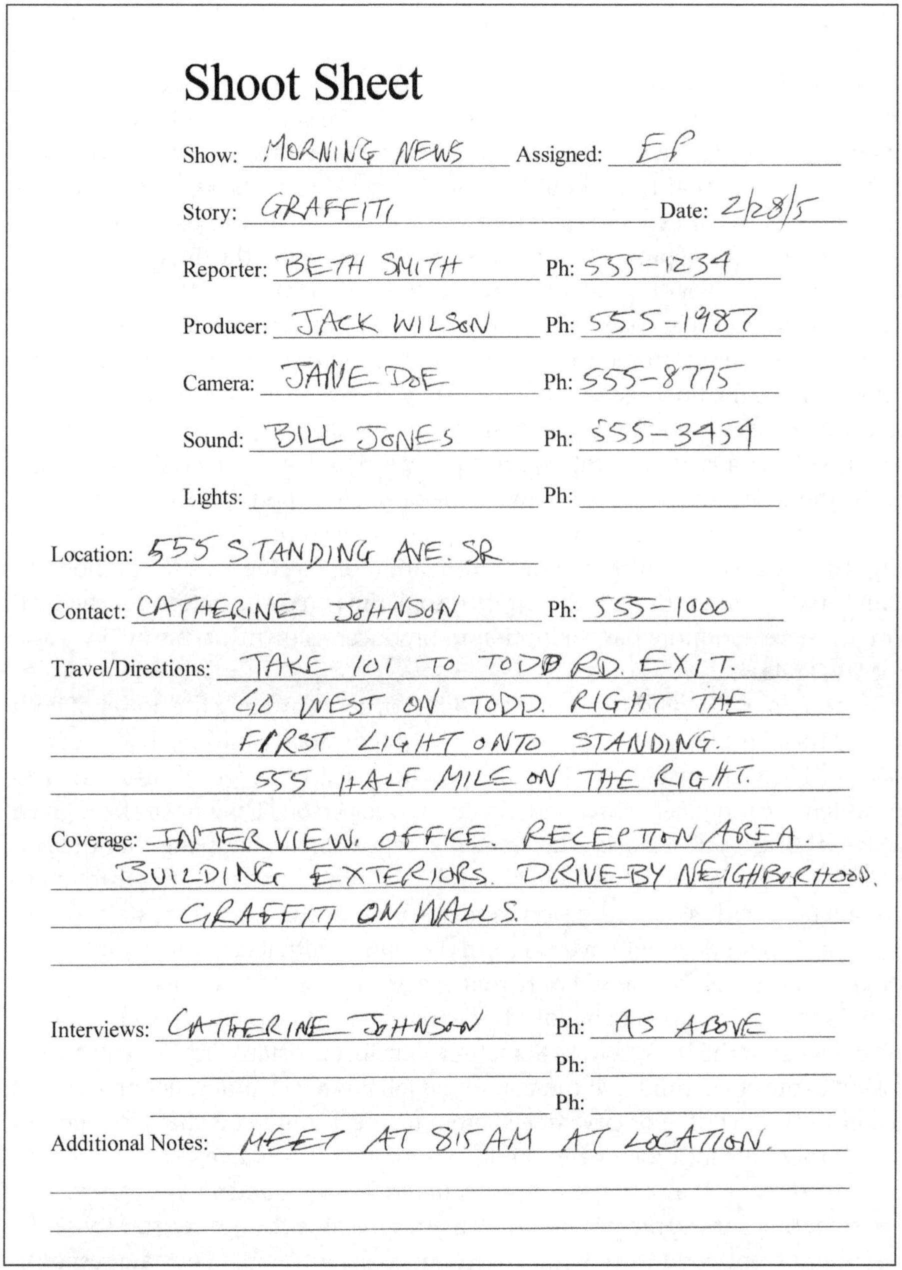

Shoot Sheet

Show: MORNING NEWS Assigned: EP

Story: GRAFFITI Date: 2/28/5

Reporter: BETH SMITH Ph: 555-1234

Producer: JACK WILSON Ph: 555-1987

Camera: JANE DOE Ph: 555-8775

Sound: BILL JONES Ph: 555-3454

Lights: _____ Ph: _____

Location: 555 STANDING AVE. SR

Contact: CATHERINE JOHNSON Ph: 555-1000

Travel/Directions: TAKE 101 TO TODD RD. EXIT. GO WEST ON TODD. RIGHT THE FIRST LIGHT ONTO STANDING. 555 HALF MILE ON THE RIGHT.

Coverage: INTERVIEW. OFFICE. RECEPTION AREA. BUILDING EXTERIORS. DRIVE-BY NEIGHBORHOOD. GRAFFITI ON WALLS.

Interviews: CATHERINE JOHNSON Ph: AS ABOVE
_____ Ph: _____
_____ Ph: _____

Additional Notes: MEET AT 8:15 AM AT LOCATION.

Figure 1.6 Typical shoot sheet

the course of the game. These ideas do not come about by accident; someone has taken the time and trouble to think about it and write them down.

The script is the blueprint that everyone works off of. It's a way of bringing all the elements of the production together so that everyone's on the same page, so to speak; so that the costume designer and the lighting camera operator have the same idea about what the movie should look like; or that the television director at the football game knows which players to focus on because those are the players that the color man has specific subjects he or she wants to comment on.

Director

This is the individual who decides how the movie is made. Everyone comes to the *director* to get their questions answered: should the scene be lit bright or dark; should the leading lady wear this dress or that one; should the actor cross the stage at this line or at that line; should the audience hear the background sound or should it be cut out; should this scene come earlier or later in the movie. Every minute detail in the production is a question answered by the director. In reality the people who work on the movie bring the director choices: this prop or that prop, this chair or that chair. The props people and the costumes designer, makeup, lighting, have all narrowed the choices down to what they see as best fitting the script, leaving the final decision to the director, who is in overall charge of the production and crew on a day-to-day basis during shooting.

The director is often involved from a very early stage in the production, often while the script is still in development. He or she is responsible for the crew and the shooting during the production stage and then is involved during the editing. The producer, and through him the distributor, has the final say on how the film is put together, though the director sometimes has the option for the final cut, or more and more has the option to produce his own cut, his own version for DVD release.

Sometimes the producer is also the director, concentrating the power of both the financial responsibility and the creative responsibility into the hands of one person. There are instances where the producer is also the writer, and instances in which the producer, writer and director is one person. Then he or she is given a special title, that of *auteur*, the French word for *author*, implying that the person is an artist in complete control of the medium from beginning through to completion, with a specific vision for every facet of the story from start to end.

The director does not have to keep a crew and cast that can number into hundreds organized all by himself or herself. He or she usually has one or more *assistant directors* to call upon to handle the crew and crowds, either onlookers or extras who appear in the background. Sometimes the first assistant director will also be tasked to direct a second unit camera, whose job it is to get atmospheric shots such as sunrises or wildlife or city streets, often the beautiful shots that intersperse a movie to set the location or time and place for a series of scenes.

The director is also assisted by a *continuity assistant* and a *script person*, who are sometimes the same person. They are responsible for the continuity of the shots and scenes and work with the technical departments. They are responsible for seeing that the correct scenes are being shot and that all the necessary material is being filmed.

In a television production, the director calls the shots to the *technical director* and gives instructions to the camera operators and sound technicians about what to shoot, when to shoot it, and how to shoot it. The technical director's job is to actually switch from one camera to another during a live production or a live-to-tape recording. The TD operates a complex piece of electronic equipment that can digitally add in special effects and graphics, which are usually created by a *CG operator* using a character generator. In this type of production the director communicates through headsets to the camera crew and also to the *floor manager*, who is in charge of operations on the studio floor itself, making sure everyone and everything is in the right position and that the performers know which camera is on air. He or she is also used to pass direction to the performers through hand signals, as well as making sure the *teleprompter operator* has the right scripts correctly queued up and ready to go.

Lighting Director

The *lighting director* is responsible for illuminating the action, but more than that, he or she is responsible for the look of the production. It's been said that photography is painting with light; this is even more true in movies, where the lighting is used to set the tone and mood of the film. At the same time the lighting has to maintain consistency and continuity from shot to shot and from scene to scene. The lighting director, also knows as the *director of photography*, or DP, is assisted by teams of electricians, called *gaffers*, who are responsible for providing the necessary power, and for placing, aiming and controlling the lamps at his or her direction.

The DP will also be in charge of the *camera operator*, who has a number of *assistant camera operators*. They make sure the camera has the aperture set as directed by the DP, that the focus is set correctly and on the right subject, and that the film path, or tape transport mechanism is working correctly and not damaging the film or tape.

The camera operators and the DP work closely with *grips*, who move the heavy equipment not only into position for each shot but often while the shot is being taken, either when the camera is mounted on a special mount such as dolly or a crane, or when the camera is mounted onto a vehicle.

Production Designer

The *production designer* sets the overall look of the movie by overseeing set design and construction, costume and makeup design, and props. This is a very important role on many movies, especially fantasy, science fiction, and other productions where the appearance of the scenes is almost as important as the scenes themselves.

Set designers are responsible for the appearance of the stage, just as a set designer would be in the theatre. In addition to designing the set, the set needs to be made practical so that cameras, camera mounts, and lights can easily be placed around it in a variety of positions. The set designers are in charge of all the construction crews necessary to create the sets, carpenters, painters, plasterers, etc.

Makeup often goes far beyond simply applying mascara and can include everything up to whole prosthetic faces, bodies, and limbs.

Costume design may be complex, fanciful creations of imagination or simple everyday wardrobe pieces. Whatever is required, it has to maintain continuity from day to day and from scene to scene regardless of when the scenes are shot. The costumes have to be kept clean, or dirty, as required.

To maintain consistency and continuity all these departments often take dozens of digital pictures to keep track of who was wearing what when, what their makeup looked like, what props they were holding, where they were sitting or standing, and even what positions their bodies were in.

Audio Recording

Recording good sound is essential to any production. If the dialog cannot be heard, or the key sound is inaudible, the scene can be ruined. The audience is much more forgiving of technical problems with the image, but problems with the audio are immediately apparent and immediately distracting. On location the *sound recordist* is responsible for getting the best-quality sound. In many instances, such as a location interview for a documentary, the sound may be more important than the picture, and the scene will be staged so as to make it possible to get the best sound recording possible, rather than creating the best possible image.

The sound recordist is assisted on location by a number of technicians, such as *boom operators*, who hold the microphone on an extended arm over the scene. The boom can be a simple, lightweight rod, or a complex mechanical arm that allows the boom operator to pivot and swing the microphone as needed.

When the shoot is finished, other teams of *audio recording technicians* get involved, usually after the picture has been edited into its final form. Here much of the sound on a major production will be recorded; whole scenes of dialog will be re-performed by the actors; effects such as footsteps, doors creaking, thunder, wind, bird sounds, gunshots, and swords clashing will be added; and everything is re-recorded and remixed together to produce the cleanest sound possible.

Editing

The *editor* takes charge of the material after it's been shot. This may be while production is still under way, or it might not be until everything is shot. He or she is responsible for assembling the material into a coherent order, cutting the shots so that they flow together, make sense, and drive the narrative forward. The editor is helped in organizing and keeping track of all the shot material by one or more *assistant editors*. They may also be responsible for cutting some scenes, or building sections of the video, particularly those that might be shot by the second unit director and crew.

It's traditional in large productions that the picture edit is finalized or locked before the project is handed to the *sound editors*, who mix together all the sounds that are heard, including the music that's either prerecorded or specially composed for the film.

All of these people aren't needed to make every video or even every film, but each of these functions will have to be done to some extent. There will always have to be someone who shoots the video, and someone who decides what shots to take, someone who records the sound, someone who edits the pictures, and someone who creates the graphics. It's possible that one person will do all of these jobs, but it's more usual for any video production to be made by a team. A team of four to six people will work best for most small productions. Ideally everyone will contribute to each phase of the production and to each of the jobs that need to be done, probably by taking turns so that everyone can gain experience in each of the functions. Obviously some students will be more drawn to some functions than others. Some may be more adept at camera work, while others might focus more on editing, and others on writing and directing.

Careers

Obviously with this many jobs to fill on any major production there are a great many careers in the film, video, and television industry. Though many of these jobs in the feature film industry are based in southern California and much of the television industry is based in New York, there are many thousands of other productions being undertaken every day, all over the country, for every conceivable need in hundreds of industries and organizations.

To succeed in a career in film or video requires talent, dedication, experience, knowledge, and a little bit of sheer good luck.

Talent is hard to quantify, but it hinges on your ability to be creative, to find new and different and imaginative ways to convey information or to tell a story. An important ability is to be able to communicate well, to explain your ideas to people, to be able to write clearly and speak coherently. These aren't specific talents, though natural ability helps, but communication skills can be learned and honed. Take every opportunity to practice writing and speaking in public.

Dedication means perseverance; it means being willing to make sacrifices and to work hard. If you are not prepared to spend the time and put the effort into learning and practicing your craft, often at the expense of other pastimes, then it would probably be better to pursue an easier career path. The more you do it, the more experience you'll get. Experience is a great teacher, and the more you can get under your belt, the more knowledge you'll gain. With more experience comes more contacts with other people in the industry. The more people you know, the more chances you'll have of finding good jobs. This is where that bit of good luck comes in.

Not every experience will be a good experience, but learn to learn from your mistakes. Part of experience is being prepared to continually assess your work, to see what could have been done better, and to do it better next time. It's important to be able to take criticism, take what's of value in the criticism, and to learn from it.

Jobs in the video industry are much sought after, which makes its a very competitive business. For most positions the minimum educational level is a college degree. It doesn't have to be a degree in broadcasting or communications, though most entry-level positions are filled from the ranks of recent film and television graduates. Oddly, the higher in the industry you go, the less important these credentials become, but for starting out these are important stepping stones.

However competitive the industry is and however competitive you have to be, it is also essential that you be able to work well as part of a team; without good teamwork and collaboration no project can be successful. It's essential that everyone who works on a team be reliable, can be counted on, and be prepared to work hard to complete every assignment and meet every deadline. Missed deadlines are not forgotten or easily forgiven in the video industry. A missed deadline can ruin a broadcast or incur enormous penalties in cost overruns.

The video industry is constantly changing. New technologies are constantly shifting the production process. Be prepared to spend your career learning new things, new techniques, new styles, and new ways of producing informative, creative, imaginative, and inspiring work.

2

Editing

The first movies were single, static shots of everyday events. The Lumière brothers' screening in Paris of a train pulling into the La Ciotat train station caused a sensation. Silent, black-and-white, it still held a gripping reality for the audience. The brothers followed this with a staged comic scene. Georges Méélièès expanded this into staging complex tableaux. It wasn't until Edwin H. Porter and D. W. Griffith in the United States discovered the power of editing one shot next to another that the movies were really born. Griffith also introduced such innovations as the flashback, the first real use of film to manipulate time. Close-ups were used to emphasize the moment of impact; wide shots were used to establish context; parallel action and other story devices were introduced, but the real discovery was that the shot is the fundamental building block of film. A film is built one shot at a time, one after the other.

Editing is at the heart of film and video production. Without editing we'd just have moving pictures. First and foremost, editing is about storytelling; it assembles content of the film and creates its structure. Editing is used to establish and develop the mood of a film, create its strength, and move its story forward. Every video of film—a fantasy trilogy many hours in length, the simplest home movie, every wedding video, training video, corporate presentation, school biology report presented on video—every one is a story. Every story should have a beginning, middle, and end, just like a well-structured essay. Every movie should progress through the basic structure of presentation, rising action, complication, climax, and finally *dénouement* or resolution, though perhaps not necessarily in that order. This is the purpose of editing, to build that structure, to use the building blocks of shots that were taken, and to construct something solid from it. That structure keeps the viewers' attention, makes them want more, and finally satisfies them by showing them a complete work which they understand and appreciate. To the extent that your video follows the dictates of good storytelling and good structure is the extent to which your video production will be successful.

One important key to the editing process is to first consider the audience that you are approaching. The audience for a wedding video is a fairly narrow group and will have different demands and expectations from another audience. The audience for the highlights video of a high school basketball season will have different expectations. Both of these audiences will have different degrees of tolerance for different subjects. The wider the audience you want to approach the more tightly you'll have to control your structure, the more you'll have to ensure that you build a sound, readily accessible, well-paced story to keep the audience watching. Whoever your audience is, your purpose as editor is to find the structure and piece it together in a way that best suits the story you want to tell. Many times it can be useful to look beyond the obvious, to look beyond simple linear chronology to find something that you can use to transform the mundane and ordinary into something exciting and entertaining, or least watchable.

Films and videos are made in the moments when one shot changes into another, when one image is replaced by the next, when one point of view becomes someone else's point of view. Without the image changing, you just have moving pictures. The Lumières' novelty would have never reached beyond the penny arcade. The idea of changing from one angle to another or from one scene to another quickly leads to the concept of juxtaposing one idea against another. It soon becomes apparent that the impact of storytelling lies in the way in which the shots are ordered.

Editing Basics

Video and film and television are a language. It's a language we are all somewhat familiar with, partly because we have been watching films and television since childhood, and partly because it is a visual language that attempts to reproduce the way we look at the world to convey information or to tell a story. What we may not be familiar with is the grammar of the language, how the language works, and why it works the way it does. You don't speak in single grunts or single words. To make sense, you have to string the words together. How you string the words, or in movies the pictures, together determines what your audience will understand.

The basic word in the language of video is a shot. In the language of film, the cut or edit between two shots is the space between two words. Usually these shots form a continuous thought or idea; sometimes, if the scene changes, the cut can also be the period at the end of a sentence. Larger blocks may be divided by different transitions, cross dissolves or wipes. Think of it as a paragraph change, the conclusion of a section. Even larger blocks like chapters might be separated by fades to black, by some special effect, or by titles to tell the audience we're moving on to something new.

Video or film production is also based on the notion of time, linear time of a fixed length. Whether it is 10 minutes, 30 minutes, one hour, two hours, or more, the idea is that the film is seen as a single event of fixed duration. On the other hand, time within the film itself is infinitely malleable. Events can happen quickly—we fly from one side of the world to another, from one era to a different century, in the blink of an eye. A man can travel from New York to San Francisco instantaneously, from one shot to the next; at one moment he can be in one city and in the next in another. Or events can happen very slowly, every detail and every angle, slowed down to be seen at far greater length than the true expanse of time, or seen again and again. Editing is the process used to create this illusion of time manipulation.

Editing is about three things: selection, arrangement, and timing. The editor's first decisions are:

1. Which shot to use

2. In what order the shots will appear

3. How long each shot will be seen

Whether the editing takes place when the writer scripts one shot and then another, or the director stages a scene so that it is put together with a certain continuity of shots, or in some moment of serendipity in the cutting room when one shot is placed next to another, that is where movies are made.

Editing is an art and a craft, and like any craft it has to be learned. Simply possessing the tools is not enough. Anyone can buy a tool belt with a hammer and all the electric tools you could ask for, but you still may not be a carpenter, let alone an artist in wood. The same is true of editing. Acquiring and learning how to use the tools is only part of the process; you also have to learn the craft and art of using the tools.

The notion of non-linear presentation of films and videos that DVD offers is antithetical to the idea of film as a progression in time. Over the years there have been many attempts to make films non-linear or with variable structures and outcomes, much like a game. None has been really successful. The reason I think is that the movies are about storytelling, and that implies the linearity of presentation. If variability is introduced to the movie, or if the film can be seen in any order, then its ethos as a story disappears. We will then all see a different story. We'll no longer be able to say, "Did you like *Casablanca*?" The question would now be, "How was your version of *Casablanca*?" Not quite the same thing, and probably not providing the same sense of satisfaction and fulfillment, which is why I think the attempts at non-linearity or variability have largely failed except in gaming itself.

I am often asked how long it takes to edit something. The only answer I can usually find is that it takes as much time as you have. The constraints of time can have several causes:

- Deadline, as in broadcast airtime, or assignment due date
- Cost, because of limitations of budget
- A combination of the two

I have worked on news pieces that should have taken an hour to edit that have been cut for air in less than ten minutes, and I have worked on pieces that could have been cut in an hour that took weeks. An edit can go on endlessly. It never really finishes; it simply stops. Painters often talk about painting in this way, that you just reach a point where the work stops and you say that's it, it's finished. Eventually you reach a point at which all your additional effort in editing isn't making it better, simply different. You're rearranging the shots, making subtle adjustments that can only be seen on the 20th viewing. It's often better to stop earlier rather than later. There is a danger in chipping away too much, in too finely honing a piece, eventually cutting into the core and damaging the material. As the editor you get used to seeing the pictures again and again. You see the content more quickly. You understand the flow of the shots more quickly, and then the danger is that you mistake your understanding and comprehension of the material for that of the audience, who has never seen the film before. This happens less often when a director has a clear vision of the picture and has been able to convey that vision. The greater danger comes when the director's concept is unclear both to him or her and to you as the editor; then the risk of overcutting increases. Directors confident about their ideas, directors who know clearly what they want, tend to shoot less, with little extra cover. Sometimes this will get them and the editor into trouble in the cutting room. But when it works, when the director's vision is clear and well-executed, the work can be very good. When it doesn't, the work tends to be mediocre. Uncertain directors tend to overshoot, giving the editor a vast choice of angles, more than they will probably want and certainly more than they will need. This is where the greatest danger comes in overcutting: putting in too many angles to fit in every vision—a bit of this, a bit of that, and in the end, not much of anything.

Because editing is so important to the production we will come back to it again and again throughout this book, but let's begin by getting familiar with the editing software you'll be using. Every software will have its own manual or resources for teaching you how to work with the application. This will not supplement that; here we'll only look at the basic principles of editing software and how to work with it.

Relational Cutting

Many shots that you cut together have no direct connection, but by simply putting them together you are implying a relationship. If you have a shot of a plane, followed by the shot of a pilot, you have created for the audience a relationship between the two. Their response will always first be that he or she is the pilot of the plane. If you have a shot of a man going into a house, even if you can't see the man clearly, and you follow that with a shot of a man coming into a house, the audience will always assume that the person you saw in the first shot is the same person as that in the second shot.

Every pair of shots will always try to force on the audience some kind of relationship. Sometimes, as in the case of the plane and the pilot, it may be obvious, and sometimes the shots may be very different. Nonetheless, the audience's first response is to try to draw a relation between the two. It may be a direct relationship, such as two people looking at each other, or it may be the relationship between ideas. The shot of a broken window followed by the shot of a child crying creates a relationship. The audience might not know what it is, but it will try to find one.

The relationship between pictures is almost more important than the pictures themselves. Putting a certain shot after another shot has a different meaning if it is placed before the other shot. The classic example is the three shots of a burning building:

A. The building on fire

B. The building exploding

C. Two men running away

In this order the audience sees it as two men escaping the exploding building. If you see A, then C, followed by B, you might think the men are trying to escape and are caught by the explosion. If you see C, then B, then A, you will probably think the men set the explosion that caused the fire.

So the sequence of shots is important. If you see the shot of boy who looks up, followed by the shot of a tree falling, the audience's response is likely to be that the boy watching the tree being cut down. If however, we see the tree falling first and then see the boy looking up, the audience is likely to think that the tree is falling on the boy.

This is *continuity* editing, arranging the shots in a sequence that suggests an order of events, one event following after another in a logical progression.

Moving Objects

Objects in motion have a special relationship in video and film production, because their very movement creates a relationship, whether intended or not, to other shots, whether they are static or have movement. When you edit together objects in motion you are establishing relationships for the audience. If you cut between objects or people who are:

- Moving towards each other, the audience anticipates a meeting or collision
- Moving in the same direction, the audience will see them as following each other, chasing each other, or going to the same destination
- Moving apart, in opposite directions, the audience will perceive them as moving away from each other

If you cut between moving and static objects, the audience has a response to the scene based on whether:

- You cut from a static shot to a shot with movement, which creates acceleration, speeding up the scene
- You cut from a shot with movement to a static shot, which creates deceleration, slowing down the scene

These are important concepts to be aware of, especially in continuity editing, where you are trying to make the flow of events as natural as possible, as in most narrative films.

There are short clips on the DVD that illustrate these cuts.

Montage

A *montage* is a French word for a series of images combined to produce an effect by association. You have all seen many montages. The opening of movies and TV shows are often done in the form of a montage. There are basically three types of montage:

- Sequential montage, in which a series of shots are seen, often in quick succession
- Multi-image montage, in which the screen is split into two, four, eight, 16 or more times, often with the images constantly changing

Figure 2.1 Multi-image montage

- Superimposed images, in which two or more images are mixed together with multiple layers of images seen by controlling opacity

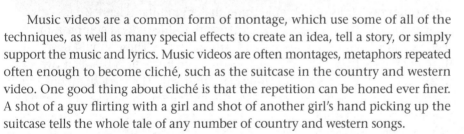

Figure 2.2 Superimposed image montage

Music videos are a common form of montage, which use some of all of the techniques, as well as many special effects to create an idea, tell a story, or simply support the music and lyrics. Music videos are often montages, metaphors repeated often enough to become cliché, such as the suitcase in the country and western video. One good thing about cliché is that the repetition can be honed ever finer. A shot of a guy flirting with a girl and shot of another girl's hand picking up the suitcase tells the whole tale of any number of country and western songs.

Montage in its weakest form is used as a quick way to convey information. The travel sequence is the most clichéd: character leaves, plane takes off, plane lands, character walks out of terminal and gets in a cab, cab pulls up at curb, character walks into a building. This is superficial montage to convey minimal information.

Another commonly used form of montage is a complex compositing effect to overlay multiple, changing images on the screen. This type of montage was popularized by the great filmmaker, theoretician, and teacher Slavko Vorkapich and is now most commonly seen in program openings and main title sequences, where it incorporates graphical elements as well as photographic ones. A classic example is the opening for the Super Bowl. A few years ago CBS created a wonderful montage in which we see small boys playing football on a lawn, then NFL stars repeating their motions in a stadium while the narration talks about a uniquely American sport, the spectacle, the fun, the camaraderie in play and performance, and the sense of celebration we experience as fans, as participants, both as children and as professionals, as Americans. It is deeply complex, emotional, full of evocative ideas and concepts, and it is brought together through images, music, and special effects. It creates a powerful, persuasive impact. Even something as simple as two shots, football player and lightning. The shots have no direct relationship, but together they form a continuity of ideas.

Montage isn't confined to documentary or music videos and is occasionally seen in feature films such as the climactic baptism scene in *The Godfather*. Here, with Bach's music and the Roman Catholic liturgy as a background, Michael Corleone literally becomes a godfather while eliminating his principal enemies. The two stories are intercut and built up together into a classic piece of cinema editing.

Jump Cuts

Editing establishes the relationship between people and objects within a scene. Shots within a scene relate to each other. Generally one shot has a relationship of content, subject or idea, or establishes a juxtaposition of ideas, two very different ideas or subjects being compared or contrasted.

A *smooth cut* is one in which the relationship between adjacent shots is obvious, apparent, and unintrusive.

A *jump cut* is an edit between shots that are mismatched. The change is disturbing; the audience's attention is disrupted, forcing them to look for a new relationship between the shots, between their content and their ideas. The jump cut is often two shots of the same thing that are similar (Figure 2.1).

On the DVD is a short video sequence that illustrates a common mistake seen in many beginners' videos; that is the jump cut. These should be avoided. In the sequence there are a number of edits. The first edit is between two shots of the Hoover Tower, a Stanford University landmark. There is a slight but abrupt change between the two shots. This is the most common cause of a jump cut, placing side-by-side shots that are similar but not the same. You get this disconcerting little jump, as if you blacked out for a fraction of a second. It suddenly pulls the viewers out from the content of the video as they say to themselves, or perhaps even out loud, "What was that?"

Figure 2.3
These two shots make a jump cut

You can also get a jump cut, seen between the second and third shots in the sequence, if you put together two very different shots, such as the shot of the tower, followed by the closer shot of the person on the platform, in the third shot. Though in the long shot the small figure of the person can be seen in the distance, cutting to a tighter shot is an abrupt change. It's disorienting because the viewer has little or no immediate reference to the relationship between the two shots. There are two typical solutions to this problem. One is done in editing, by placing a cross dissolve between the shots as we see in the sequence. A better solution is provided by the camera operator who gives us the shot that goes from the long shot and pushes into the closer shot. Without these transitional aids, the shots appear to the audience to jump.

Another type of jump cut is that caused by discontinuity in shooting: an actor is wearing a jacket in one shot but not in the next; someone is holding an object in their right hand in one shot and in their left in the next; any sudden change in posture, costume, expression, or any sudden repositioning of foreground or background objects may appear to be jump cuts.

The general rule is that jump cuts should not be used if you can help it. Or use them so often that it becomes your style. Then it's art.

How Long Is Long Enough?

How long should a shot be on the screen? The shots in the jump cut sequence are quite short. The purpose is to illustrate the edit, not to really look at the contents of the shots. Nonetheless, normally a static shot, either a close-up or medium shot, needs to be on the screen a much shorter time than a long shot in which the audience is following a movement. Take a look at the length shots on the DVD. The first shot that pans with the electric cart is almost 13 seconds long, while the second, static shot is not even seven seconds long. You can watch the first longer than you'd like to look at the second.

Though there is no hard and fast rule, generally shots without dialog remain on the screen no more than six to eight seconds on television with its small screen. In feature films shots can be held for quite a bit longer because the viewer's eye simply has a lot more traveling to do to take in the full scope of the image. This is probably why movies seem much slower on the television screen than they do in the theater. While a close-up can be on the screen quite briefly, a long shot will often contain a great deal of information and needs to be held longer so that your viewer has time for his or her eye to rove around it.

A shot that has been seen before, a repeat, can be on the screen quite briefly for the audience to get the information. A moving shot, such as a pan, you can often hold longer because the audience is basically looking at two shots, one at the beginning and the other at the end. If the movement is well shot, a fairly brisk move of no more than about five seconds, you can also cut it quite tightly. All you need to show is a brief glimpse of the static shot, the movement, and then cut out as soon as the camera settles at the end of the move.

If you have a shot of a watch and you're talking about the watch, the construction, the dial, the workmanship, the details, the shot could be 20 or 30 seconds. If the shot of the watch is to see the time, the shot would probably not be more than two or three seconds.

So how long should a shot be is depend on a number of factors:

1. How much do you want the viewer to see? If you want to viewer to look at the contents of the shot in detail, you should hold it on the screen longer; if you simply want them to register what the content of the shot is, then it can be on the screen briefly.

2. How quickly can you get the information across? If the shot is complex, with a lot of objects and people in the shot, it may need to be on the screen longer for the audience to get the information; if the shot is the word NO in white letters against a black background, the shot will register quickly.

3. How familiar you are with the material? If the audience has seen the shot before, the second time it sees it the shot doesn't have to be on the screen as long.

4. How much action, movement, or change is in the shot? As we've seen, shots with movement can be held on the screen longer than shots without movement or change in the content. If the content is constantly changing the shot can be held for quite some time.

5. How good is the picture, strong the composition, or beautiful the image? Powerful images with strong compositions or beautiful scenes or objects or people can be held on the screen longer than mundane shots. A gorgeous sunset can be on the screen longer than the same shot at midday. A shot that is boringly composed from an ordinary angle should not be on the screen as long as a shot that's a forceful composition taken from an interesting angle.

Think of how you look at a scene when you walk into a room. You look at it in pieces, in single shots, maybe a wide shot that shows you the whole room, followed perhaps by a closer look at someone you know, then a picture of someone else who has called out to you. You watch them speak, then you look at someone else who responds. Your eyes move around the room, but you really only see the single images you want to look at. If someone shows you something, like their new watch, you see the watch as if it's a close shot, the watch, the person's wrist and very little else. Then you might look up at the person to see their reaction. We really tend to look at the world in closer shots rather than long shots. We'll talk about this more in the next chapter.

Compression and Expansion of Time

Because films and video are based on specific lengths of time, the events within the video are usually condensed in time. This can be in broadest sense such as in a story that covers days, weeks, months or even years; but it is also compressed in a narrow sense, often within each scene. We see it in practically every film. A woman gets behind the wheel of a car, and a moment later the vehicle pulls away from the curb. She has put on her seat belt instantly, the car has started instantly, and it's been put into gear instantly.

The only time in movies that starting a car takes a protracted amount of time, fumbling with keys, grinding gears, stalling, etc. is when Godzilla is coming down the street.

There are many ways to contract time in a video, to speed things up. Simple processes can be condensed into a couple of quick shots that illustrate the essence of what's being done, making a meal for instance, or fixing a flat tire, or writing an e-mail message, or of course going from one place to another.

Suspense on the hand often works to expand time, to take what should be only a few moments and make it seem to last longer. This can be done with slow motion, but it can also be done by simply using a variety of shots that take more than the actual time to develop the continuity of events. The classic example is a bomb placed in a crowded location. We see the people moving around, we see the bomb ticking down, we see someone coming to defuse it. Intercutting these three elements heightens tension. The trick is to draw out the time to increase the suspense without stretching it so far as to seem absurd. When it's done well, with well-composed, dynamic shots the effect can be very powerful. When done poorly, it can look just silly.

Cutting Rhythm

An edit works well when it is motivated by something, either by something happening within the scene, or by an external sound, such as music, narration, or dialog. Much of editing is driven by the editing of sound, with the picture cut to the pace and rhythm of the sound. This can be the cadence of a narrator's speech, or much more obviously the rhythm of music. When you are cutting to a musical score, the rhythm and pace of the music dictates where an edit should take place.

Another important consideration for where an edit takes place is movement. It is always better to cut during a movement of the subject, rather than while a subject is static. This does not mean a camera movement. Avoid cutting during a camera movement. If there is movement within the frame, a person rising from chair, picking up a phone, opening a door, turning around, any movement like this within the frame will often provide a better cut point than when the subject is still.

Another important reason for cutting is for a change in composition. Changing between dynamically different compositions can create tension. Use of composition, tone, or color will often determine the choice of shot as well as how often you cut. The faster the cuts the more tension is heightened. A series of shots with strong, dynamically opposed compositions, tones, or colors will build up a cumulative response, adding to each shot, increasing tension. This works particularly if the shots are fresh. The more often shots are repeated the more the impact will be lessened.

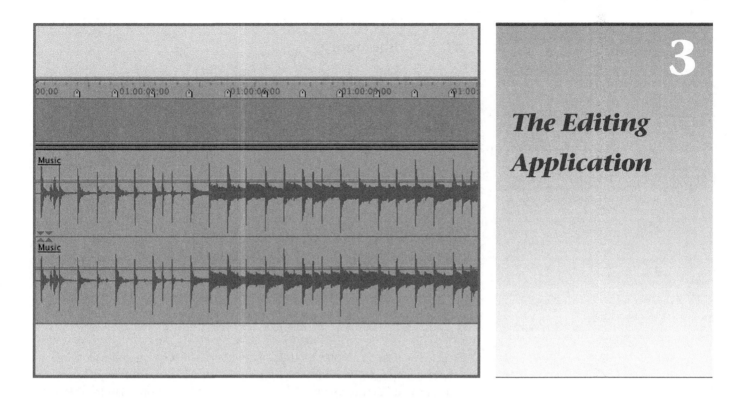

3

The Editing Application

*E*very non-linear video editing system has a window that serves as a means of organizing your material. Whether it's called the Project window as in Premiere Pro (Figure 3.1a) or the Browser in Final Cut Pro (Figure 3.1b), it serves as a list of the material you have to work with. This window should give you the ability to create folders or bins in which you can move material to organize it based on content. This window will usually provide information about the media you have to work with, how long it is, what type of media file it is, any timecode information associated with it, and often much, much more.

Every editing system will have some way for you to look at your video, usually in a separate window, sometimes called the Source monitor or the Viewer. Additionally there'll be a Timeline for laying out your video and audio in the order in which you want them to play back. The output of the Timeline window will usually display in a separate window, sometimes called the Record monitor

Figure 3.1a Premiere Pro Project window

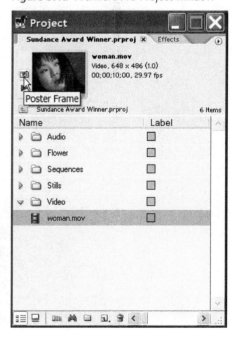

Figure 3.1b Final Cut Pro Browser

	Name	Duration	In	Out	Media Start
	Pagoda.jpg	00:00:10:00	00:01:00:00	00:01:09:29	00:00:00:00
	San Francisco	00:07:30:02	Not Set	Not Set	00:11:19;14
	Sequence 1	00:00:46;29	Not Set	Not Set	01:00:00;00
	Track 03.aif	00:03:23;10	Not Set	Not Set	00:00:00;00

What Is Timecode?

Timecode is a series of numbers that are written on your videotape whenever you make a DV recording or record on a camcorder. The numbers represent time and on most consumer cameras begin at 00:00:00:00, zero hours, zero minutes, zero seconds, and zero frames. On higher-end and professional cameras the start number can be set to anything you like. A timecode number is assigned to every frame of video, in the European PAL system 25 frames per second, in the North American and Japanese NTSC system 30 frames per second.

For NTSC this is a problem, because the true frame rate of all NSTC video isn't 30fps but 29.97fps. Because of this NTSC has created two ways of counting timecode called drop frame and non-drop frame.

Non-drop frame displays the numbers based on a simple 30fps frame rate. The problem with this is that when your timecode gets to the one-hour mark, one hour of real-world time hasn't passed yet. It's still almost four seconds from completing the hour.

Drop frame uses a complex method of counting which compensates for the difference between 29.97fps and 30fps. No frames of video are dropped. DF drops two frames a minute in its count, except every 10th minute. This means that at the one-minute mark, your DF video will go from 59;29 to 1:00;02. There is no 1:00;00 or 1:00;01. Notice the semicolons. The convention is to write DF timecode with semicolons, or at least one semicolon, while NDF is written only with colons.

The DV standard uses drop frame timecode as its counting method, though some prosumer and all professional cameras are switchable between the two.

or the Canvas in Final Cut Pro. Two typical interfaces can be seen in Figures 3.2a and 3.2b.

To play the video there are usually buttons for Play, Fast Forward, and Rewind. For complex software applications it's always a good idea to try to learn the keyboard shortcuts, as these are the most efficient ways of working with them. One of the most common keyboard shortcuts, which is almost universal to video editing applications is the spacebar to play a clip. Spacebar will usually also stop the clip. Other common keys are the J, K, and L keys. These are your VCR controls. L is the play button; K is the pause button; and J is play backwards. Usually pressing the L key repeatedly will fast-forward through your material, while pressing J repeatedly will rewind. J, K, and L were chosen because they are directly below the I and O keys. These keys are used to mark the points at which you want the shot to start, the in-point (I), and the point at which you want the shot to end, the out-point (O). Now you already know six important keyboard shortcuts; every appli-

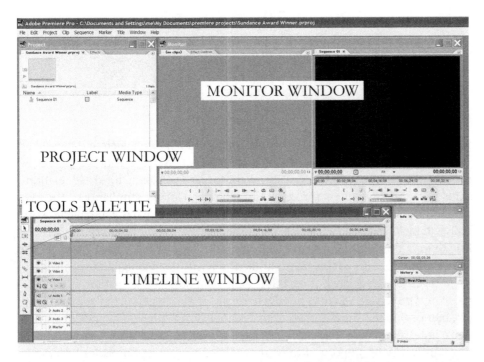

Figure 3.2a Premiere Pro interface

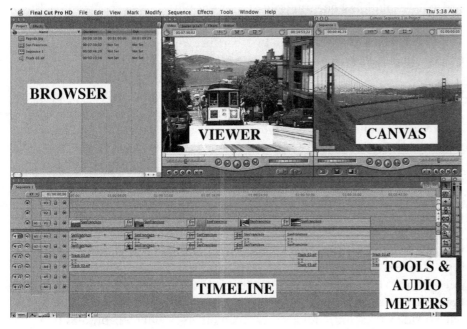

Figure 3.2b Final Cut Pro interface

cation will have its own collection. If you're going to be editing seriously, take the time to learn these shortcuts.

The first stage of editing is to look through your material and break it down into shots, organize it, arrange it into bins or folders, rename clips, add notes, and so on. This is all critical if you're working on a project that's longer than 10 minutes or so, or a project with a lot of material regardless of its finished length.

This process of viewing and logging and organizing and familiarizing yourself with the material should not be skimped or rushed or dismissed as drudge work; it is crucial to the editing process.

Look Before You Cut

When you're breaking down your material and sorting it into folders and bins what you're really doing is looking through your material. What you should watch for is relationships, shots that can easily be cut together. Looking for these relationships is critical as you look through your material. Getting familiar with the material is an important part of the editing process, learning what you have to work with and looking for cutting points. Many editors like to put the shots into a Timeline to look through them, and others prefer to look at individual items in the Source monitor. Some editors like to immediately create small sequences and group them together, not finely honed, but roughly laid out, so that first important impression is preserved. You may not use it, or any of that material, in your final project, but assembling shots quickly into a sequence is a quick and efficient way to make notes about your material.

This is why it's important to work with professional applications that allow you to have multiple sequences open at the same time. In these applications Timelines normally tab together into a single window. Some will allow you to pull the Timelines apart so that you can see two sequences on the screen at the same time, letting you pull shots from one sequence into another.

While you edit, you just put together the shots you want to work with—edit them, rearrange them, shorten, and lengthen them how you like. You can park your edited sequence to be used later, either as an edited group of shots or as a holding bin for a group of shots, but unlike a simple bin, the shots are laid out in the specific order you have arranged. The final scene is then made up by selecting shots from multiple open Timelines and moving them to the final sequence. This way of working is best with large computer monitors.

There are many different ways to work, perhaps as many different ways as there are editors. Probably the longer the project, the more variations in work flow. How you organize your material is critical in long-form production. Many people like to work in organized folders; some prefer to work with multiple sequences with few bins or folders. Others prefer to work with multiple folders, all of them open at once, either in icon view or list view. Others like to use the Find tool, leaving multiple lists open at the same time. As you become more experienced, you'll find yourself working with some methods more than others. You'll probably also find that on different projects you work in different ways. Some material lends itself to working with multiple sequences; other material might not. Some work flows are faster than others. Laying out clips in bins that you trim in the Viewer or Source monitor and then rearranging as a storyboard might sound good, but cutting up and rearranging material entirely in a Timeline is probably a lot quicker for small amounts of material.

Editing Functions

All editing applications will have ways to mark where a shot will start and where it will end, marking the in-points and out-points, usually with buttons or with the I and O keyboard shortcuts or some other keyboard shortcut. Usually this is done in the Source monitor. Many editors like to do this on the fly, while the clip is playing. This is easy for marking out-points. You're looking at the material play through the shot you want to use, and you press the keyboard shortcut at the moment you think the shot should end. This has the advantage of allowing you to judge the pace of the shot, to do it almost tactilely, to feel the rhythm of the shot. After a few tries you'll probably find you're hitting the out-point consistently on the same frame. Marking the in-point is a little different, because as you look at the material playing, you are looking at the pictures before the shot you want to use. Often you want to mark the in-point just before an action like a camera movement begins, but judging on the fly how far in front of the action to begin is a little difficult. So what a lot of editors like to do is mark the in-point while the video is playing backwards. By playing it backwards you see where the action begins and you get to judge the pace of how far before the action you want the edit to occur. If you want the edit to happen in the middle of the action, then you might make the in-point cut while playing forwards.

Marking in-points and out-points are the primary edit functions in the Source monitor or Viewer. There will then be an edit function, either by dragging a clip, clicking a button, or pressing a keyboard shortcut to bring the material in your Timeline or sequence. There are two primary edits that are most commonly used to get material precisely into the Timeline, an overwrite edit, which goes over anything that's already in the Timeline, wiping it out, or an insert edit, which puts a

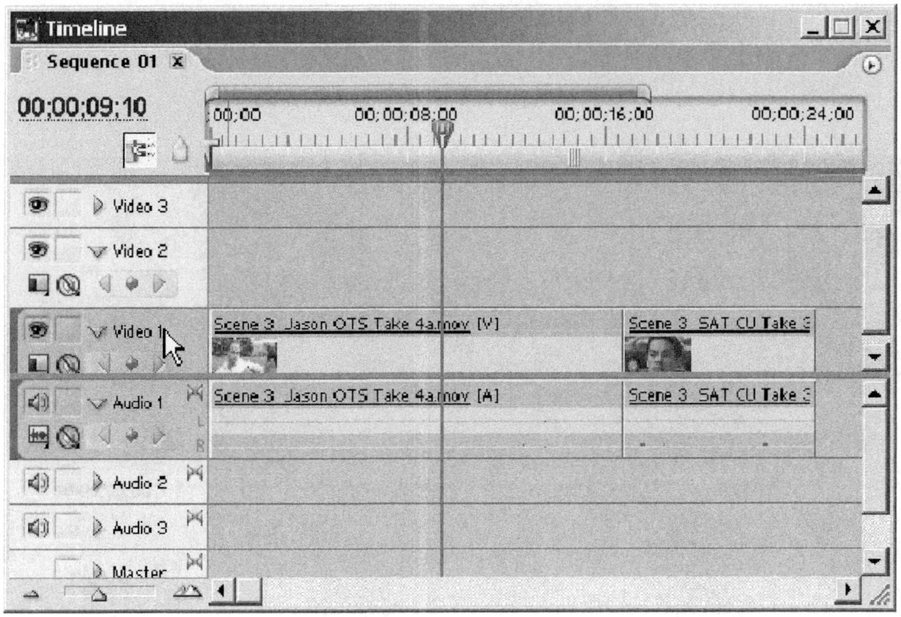

Figure 3.3a Premiere Pro track selection

Figure 3.3b Final Cut Pro patch panel

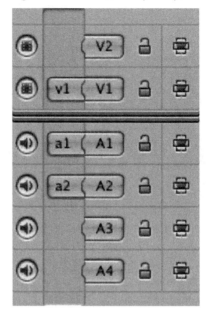

shot into the middle of a sequence and pushes everything that comes after it out of the way to make room for it. The overwrite or insert edits are usually done where the playhead, or CTI (current time indicator) is placed in the sequence. The edit will go onto whichever tracks are currently selected as destination or target tracks with the controls at the head of the Timeline (Figure 3.3a and 3.3b). Professional editing systems always allow you to have multiple tracks of video and audio to work with.

Every editing system will have other important edit functions, such as a Replace function, which will replace one shot in the Timeline with another. The application may also have a Superimpose function, which will edit a shot or a title onto an overlay track.

Trimming Your Sequence

All professional editing applications will have a number of important editing functions that allow you to modify your sequence. There will be a lift edit or delete edit which will remove an edit from its place in the Timeline. There will also be a function to perform a ripple delete, which allows you to remove a shot from a sequence and pull up everything that comes after it to fill the hole created by the removed shot, to ripple the sequence.

To trim individual shots or pairs of shots in a sequence there are four essential trim functions allowing you to perform ripple edits, roll edits, slip edits and slide edits. These can either be done numerically or more usually with a special tool for each function, sometimes in the Timeline window itself, or in a special Trim Edit window (Figure 3.4a and Figure 3.4b).

A ripple edit moves an edit point up and down the Timeline by pushing or pulling all the material on the track, shortening or lengthening the whole sequence. In a ripple edit, only one clip changes duration, getting longer or shorter.

Figure 3.4a Premiere Trim window

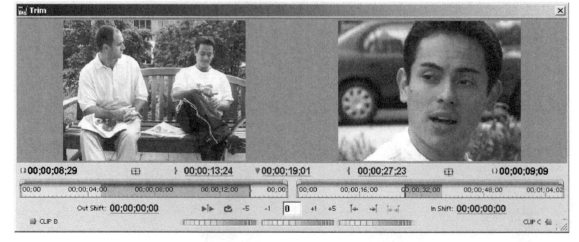

Figure 3.4b FCP's Trim Edit window

Everything else that comes after it in the track adjusts to accommodate it. In Figure 3.5a the edit is being rippled to the left, and everything after it moves to accompany it. A word of caution about rippling. If you're working with material that's cut to narration or music, rippling will easily upset the timing of the sequence, as it's pulling and pushing the entire track and its sync sound. So what's working for you at this moment in the edit may be ruining something else further down the Timeline. In these cases, the Roll tool may work better for you.

A roll edit moves an edit point up and down the Timeline between two adjacent shots. Only those two shots have their durations changed. While one gets longer, the adjacent shot gets shorter to accommodate it. The overall length of the track remains unchanged. In Figure 3.5b the edit point itself can be moved either left or right. The Roll tool acts on both shots, extending one shot while shortening the other. While the Ripple tool changes the enter length of the sequence by moving everything up and down the line, the Roll tool only affects the two adjacent shots.

A slip edit changes the in-point and out-points of a single clip. The duration of the clip remains the same, and all the clips around it remain the same. Only the in-point and out-point of the slipped clip change. If more frames are added on the front, the same amount are cut off the end, and vice versa. In Figure 3.5c the contents of the change by changing in-points and out-points, but neither its position in the sequence nor either of the adjacent shots are affected.

A slide edit moves a clip forward or backward along the Timeline. The clip itself, its duration, in-points, and out-points remain unchanged. Only its position on the Timeline, earlier or later, shortens and lengthens the adjacent shots as it slides up and down the track. In Figure 3.5d the central clip *Food4* can slide

Figure 3.5a Ripple edit

Figure 3.5c Slip edit

Figure 3.5b Roll edit

Figure 3.5d Slide edit

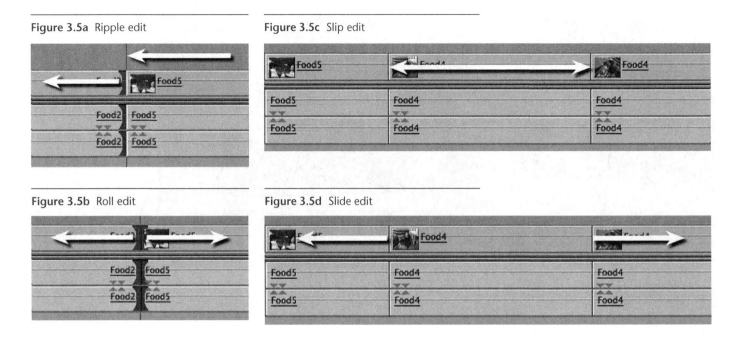

up and down the Timeline. The shot itself isn't altered, only the two adjacent shots are. The Slide tool doesn't change anything in the clip you're working on; it simply grabs the clip and pulls it forward or backward along the Timeline.

Adding Transitions

Transitions can add life to a sequence, ease a difficult edit into something smoother as we've seen, or give you a way to mark a change of time or place. The traditional grammar of film that audiences still accept is that dissolves denote small changes, while a fade to black followed by a fade from black mark a greater passage of time. With the introduction of digital effects, any imaginable movement or contortion of the image to replace one with another quickly became possible—and were quickly applied everywhere, seemingly randomly, to every possible edit. They can be hideously inappropriate, garish, and ugly. Transitions can be used effectively, or they can look terribly hackneyed. Final Cut Pro and Premiere Pro give you the option to do either or anything in between.

The most commonly used transition is a simple cross dissolve. To change between locations, a wipe or push can be effective. To indicate a longer change in time as well as place, a fade to black is often used. An iris can be useful to reveal a specific part of a scene first. Page peels are also commonly used for specific applications, as well as gradient wipes, which combine with grayscale images to produce powerful and customizable effects. These and a few other commonly used transitions, as well as some unusual ones, can be seen in the Transitions movie on the Chapter 3 portion of the DVD.

Figure 3.6 Overlap for transition

All modern video editing applications allow you to add transitions inline. That means the transition is placed between two clips that are on the same track, adjacent to each other. How the application deals with the transition is crucial to being able to add them to your Timeline correctly. Some applications will pull material from the adjacent shots to make room for the overlap required for the transition. This will shorten the sequence, making precise editing difficult. Professional editing systems such as Premiere Pro and Final Cut Pro don't do this. They require that additional media beyond the marked edit points, called handles, be available to make the transition. If there isn't sufficient media to execute the transition, the application will produce an error message.

Why does this happen? The answer is simple. The shots must overlap because frames from both shots must appear on the screen simultaneously. There needs to be extra media available to create the overlap for the transition, as shown in Figure 3.6. The pale shot on the left has to overlap the dark shot on the right by half the length of the transition, and vice versa. If that media does not exist, you can't do the transition. The application usually assumes as a default that the transition will take place centered around the marked edit point. Therefore, to execute a one-second transition, which is usually the default duration, you will need at least half a second, 15 frames, of available media after the out-point on the outgoing shot, and 15 frames in front of the in-point of the incoming shot. Unless you think of it ahead of time, and many times you don't, you'll have to deal with it when you're fine-tuning your edit. Often you'd rather not deal with transitions while you're laying out your sequence, leaving them until you've laid out the shot order.

The default transition in most applications will be the cross dissolve, and there will always be a keyboard shortcut to apply it to an edit point. It'll be one of the more useful keyboard shortcuts you can learn. Even if you're going to change the transition, it's often good to apply one just to see what a transition will look like on an edit. On many systems the cross dissolve is a real-time transition, which is another reason to apply it first, rather than a complex, fancy one that might need to be rendered.

Rendering

After you've entered a transition, you may have to render it, depending on the speed of your computer system. Some systems will be capability of real-time playback of effects like transitions, while others will not.

What rendering means is that the application has to create media for a portion of your video where none exists. Most of the two shots in your sequence are on your hard drive, but not the 30 frames that make up this one-second cross dissolve, during which one shot is changing into the other. All you've done is give the computer instructions to create that media. If you have to render the material to see the transition, the computer will create a small piece of media that it stores on your hard drive and plays back whenever you play across the transition. If you change the transition, you will probably have to re-render the effect.

Adding Titles

Every program is enhanced with graphics, whether they are a simple opening title and closing credits or elaborate motion-graphics sequences illuminating some obscure point that can best be expressed in animation. This could be simply a map with a path snaking across it or a full-scale 3D animation explaining the details of how an airplane is built. Obviously, the latter is beyond the scope of most editing applications alone, but many simpler graphics can be easily created within the editing application or some accompanying software. These include the standard animations, rolls or scrolls (vertical movement), or crawls (horizontal movement), as well as other special animations like a typewriter effect.

Fonts and Size

The most important thing to understand about creating graphics for video is the great limitations the medium puts on you. The color range and brightness range of a television display is very limited compared to computer systems. Nor are all fonts suitable for use on television. You can't just pick something you fancy and hope it will work for you. One of the main problems with video is its interlacing. Because video is made up of thin lines of information—the odd lines making up one field and the even lines the other field—each line is essentially switching on and off 30 times a second. If you happen to place a thin horizontal line on your video that falls on one of those lines but not the adjacent line, that thin, horizontal line will be switching on and off at a very rapid rate, appearing to flicker. The problem with text is that a lot of fonts have thin horizontal lines called serifs, the little footer that some letters sit on (Figure 3.7a).

Performance

Figure 3.7a Serif fonts

Performance

Figure 3.7b Sans-serif fonts

Unless you're going to make text of a fairly large size, it's generally best to avoid serif fonts. You're better off using a sans-serif font for most video work (Figure 3.7b). Interlace flickering caused by serifs and other fine lines can be alleviated somewhat by smearing the image across the interlace lines. It is easiest to do this with text created in Photoshop or some other image editing software, where you can apply a one-pixel vertical motion blur. You don't have to soften the whole image like this. If there are particular portions that appear to flicker, you can select them with a marquee or lasso, slightly feathered, and apply the vertical motion blur to just that portion of the image.

You should probably avoid small fonts as well. Video resolution is not very high, the print equivalent of 72dpi. You can read printed text in 10 point comfortably, but a 10-point line of text on television would be an illegible smear. I generally never use font sizes below 24 and prefer to use something larger.

Color and Luminance

Televisions have a pretty limited ability to reproduce color and cannot do it with the full range of millions of colors that can be done on computer screen. The same applies to the luminance (brightness) of the image. Generally when working with titles it is best to use RGB colors. Many video applications require this for images created in applications like Photoshop or Illustrator. Computer graphics usually display color values in red, green, and blue from zero to 255, a range of 256 units. For video it is best to keep the RGB values so that no value goes below 16 or above 235. If red, green, and blue are all 16, the text will look black on a TV set; similarly if the values are all 235, the video will look white. If full values of 255 are used there is a good chance the video will bloom or smear into adjacent video.

Avoid using high chrominance (color) values such as pure red or yellow. Generally a value of Red 200 with Green 16 and Blue 16 will produce bright red on a television display. Similarly a good yellow color can be created using Red 200, Green 200, with Blue 16.

To help separate text from the background video or image it's generally useful to make sure the text color and luminance value contrasts with the background. Additionally, to help this separation, it often helps to apply an edge or outline to the letters. A drop shadow can also help to improve the legibility of video text. Drop shadows are important to give the image some depth and separation. It would be quite useful for our text where the white of the letters is over the bright highlights. Another trick is to use a black color matte behind the text. Keep it to just the size of the text and reduce the opacity down to 10 or 20 percent, creating a translucent shadow area behind the text.

Safe Title Area and Safe Action Area

Televisions have a mask on the edge that cuts off some of the displayed picture area. What you see on your computer monitor is not what you get—far from WYSIWYG—and can vary substantially from television to television. That is why most titling software is marked with a Safe Action Area and a still smaller area that is defined as the Safe Title Area (Figure 3.8). It's a good idea to try to keep titles within the Safe Title Area.

Other features that can be controlled in most titling software are tracking, which is the spacing between the letters of the text, kerning, which is the spac-

Figure 3.8 Safe action and safe title areas

ing between individual letter pairs, and leading (pronounced *ledding*, as in little bits of lead spacing used in hot metal typesetting), which is the spacing between lines of text.

Often editing applications will have basic animation capabilities, which will allow you to move text on and off the screen in a great number of different ways.

Music

Music videos are the staple of MTV, VH1, and CMT. Every popular music recording artist has a video made to accompany their music. It's an essential ingredient in artist and record promotion. The key point to remember about editing music videos is that it's about the music. Everything is dictated by the rhythm, the tone, and texture of the music—whether you're working on a project that will be created entirely from computer-generated animation or from a multi-camera shoot of a performance—where the edit point comes on each shot is driven by the beat of the music.

This may well be your first exercise in editing video, but with a good non-linear editing application, this will be a great way to get the sense of how the rhythm of music and video can bring together different elements, juxtaposing them and creating new meanings where perhaps none existed before.

Marking the Beat

To edit music, the first step you need to take is to find the beat, the rhythm of the music and mark it. Most video editing applications will allow you to do this by adding markers to your clip or to the Timeline, or both. If you have to add the markers to the Timeline, simply place your music track into the sequence and add the markers on the beat. Many applications will let you add markers on the fly, tapping a keyboard shortcut to add a marker as the music plays (Figure 3.9).

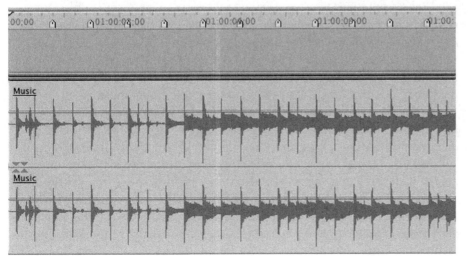

Figure 3.9 Music markers

Once you get into the groove of it, you can quickly clean up your markers till they're exactly placed. Now that you've marked up, you're ready to start laying in picture. If you to want to use any natural or sync sound with your music video, you might want to add a couple of tracks and move the music down, leaving the primary tracks free for the sync sound that goes with the video.

It's a good idea to lock your music tracks. Your music track shouldn't be going anywhere, and you don't want to accidentally delete it or overwrite it when you put in some video.

Once you've got the markers set, either in the Timeline or on the clip itself, you can use them as guides to where to make your edits. You don't have to make an edit at every beat, right on every marker, but it is a simple way to put together video that works well with the music. Use the markers as a guide to where you can place an edit.

There are basically two ways to edit to the music: either the cut is on the beat, or the event in the shot is on the beat. By putting the cut on the marker you're cutting *on the beat*. This is the most common form of cutting to music, and you'll see it every day in any video that has music. This works especially well for shots that are static or aren't dynamic within themselves, shots that don't have strong movement or forceful action. This works pretty well and will always produce acceptable, if predictable, results. Placing the cut on the beat works especially well for stills or other images without much action.

However, if there is strong action in the shot, it's often better to cut *off the beat*. Often the material itself might have a strong action in it, like a door slamming shut, a hand banging a table, a guitar chord being struck, or any other forceful action. If you want to match the strong action, say the door slam to the music, then the action needs to be on the marker where the beat is. To see that action, the edit then takes place off the beat, on either side of the marker, leaving the action on the beat. Take the example of a shot of a drummer striking his drum. If you're cutting on the beat, you're cutting to or away from the drum on the very frame on which it's struck. The strike on the drumhead explodes the edit into the next shot. However, to see the drummer beat the drum, you really need to cut off the beat so that the edit occurs in the gaps between strikes. This way the action is placed on the moment of the beat. When you have strong action like this, these are all moments that need to be seen. The impact event should happen on the beat; the edit, hidden between the beats. No video will have just one or the other, on the beat or off the beat, which would make it horribly monotonous, but a mixture of the two, changing back and forth through the rhythm of the music and of the images.

Though the markers will probably be regular, it's not a good idea to maintain the same pace throughout the music video. A fast pace will wear on the audience and soon lose its impact. A slow pace will bore the audience. Generally editors like to use a mix of faster-paced sections, especially at the beginning to get the audience excited and involved, then to reduce the tempo, let the audience enjoy the content, but returning to the faster tempo periodically to bring the audience back into the energy of the movie or just to wake them up. This pacing of fast and slow, tension and release, is the real art of movie making, directing and especially editing.

Editing is so much about rhythm and cadence, both of which are dictated by sound, whether it's music or a narrator's voice and rhythm of speech. Music is about repetition, passages, and choruses that often repeat. Using your editing system you can create a sequence that repeats for each chorus. You may not want each chorus to be exactly the same, but have small variations, though the structure and rhythm and many of the shots may repeat. Most professional editing systems will allow you to duplicate sequences, as many as you need, and make the variations on them. You can then combine the sequences with other material in a finished Timeline.

These are just some of the features available in most non-linear editing applications, and getting experience and confidence with the software is as important as getting to understand and appreciate how shots work together and interact with each other and with the accompanying audio. The music exercise is a good way to get a handle on all these concepts: shots, rhythm, juxtaposition, interaction, transitions, and titles.

Exercise: Music Video

Throughout this book you'll find exercises and projects that will give you practice in the skills you need to move forward with learning video production techniques. Every chapter will end with a project for you to do. At the end of this chapter, we're having an exercise and project one after the other. Think of an exercise as a shorter project, something to practice on, while a project might be something you'd want to have shown on your school or local access television channel.

The first exercise is to create a music video. You should now be comfortable working with the software application you're using. You should know how to put clips into the sequence, edit them, add transitions, and do basic titling.

You should work in small groups, depending on the availability of computers and facilities. Ideally groups should be from two to four students for this exercise.

1 For the exercise you should work with supplied footage. This may be footage shot by or provided by your instructor. It may also come from sources that have been digitized or prepared for the project.

2 The group should pick a one-to-two-minute section of a song that can be used with the video elements. The music must be suitable for a campus environment and must not contain any sounds or lyrics that are indecent, abusive, vulgar, or offensive in any sexual, racial, cultural, or ethnic context.

3 Using the techniques you've learned, edit the picture and sound. Use markers on the music to define the beat and where you want the edits to occur.

4 Add transitions and titles as necessary. Make sure there is an opening title as well as closing credits at the end of the video.

This is an exercise, not a project, as it will probably use copyrighted music and cannot be viewed or distributed for any kind of public performance. If you want to show your finished videos publicly, copyright clearances for the music and for synchronization will have to be obtained.

Project: Biographies

This project incorporates still images, narration, and titles to create a short biography that tells your audience something about the members of your team, who they are, where they live, their family, friends, and special interests. This should be a fun project, because it's a subject you know well and it's something that can be enjoyed by all your friends, classmates, and family members.

Again, as in all the exercises and projects, you'll probably want to work in small groups depending on the available of facilities and the size of the class.

Groups should probably be from three to five students. It's a bit more fun with a slightly larger group. If the students cannot create productive groups the instructor will do it for you.

1 Students should bring photographs of themselves, their families, friends, and surroundings. This is easiest if the stills are digital; if not they can be brought in as prints. The picture should cover a variety of periods of your lives from a young child until the present.

2 The images can either be scanned or videotaped by mounting them on a copy stand. Scanning the images provides more options for sizing and creating motion to make the video more interesting.

3 Each person in the group should write a short narration that explains briefly the images and tells your audience who you are and what's important in your life.

4 Record the narration, either to tape first, or the computer, either in your editing application or a sound recording application.

5 Edit the pictures and narration together. The video does not have to have each student in sequence. You could say something about everyone's families first, then something about everyone's interests, sports, or hobbies. Try to make the combination of pictures and sound as interesting as possible.

6 Add transitions, but keep it simple. Don't fill the video with garish digital effects.

7 Add opening and closing credits, or even titles during the video to define sections or to explain the contents.

8 You can add some music, but it must be royalty-and copyright-free music (music legally available on the web), buy out music (which gives you rights to the music for your video productions), or music you have created, perhaps using Soundtrack or GarageBand or other software, or music you have performed and recorded.

When the projects are completed they will be viewed by the class and shown to a wider audience if possible.

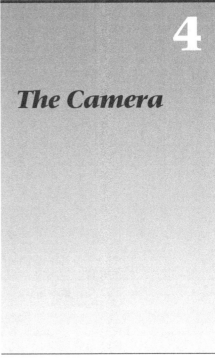

The Camera

4

Now that you appreciate the importance of pacing and shot juxtaposition it's time to learn how to get those shots, good shots that make a compelling video. Camera operators who don't know how to edit or how a video should be put together will never really be good camera operators. It's far too common to see material from an excellent videographer who knows how to expose perfectly and craft beautiful images but doesn't know how they go to together, often producing material which is basically unusable from an editor's point of view. For a film or video to be effective requires not only that it's cut well but also that it's shot in a way that it *can* be cut well. Not only should the material be well shot, and beautifully shot, but the camera operator should be constantly aware that no matter how perfectly a shot is lit and composed, if it cannot be edited with the shots and doesn't contribute to the narrative, it will be pointless and probably end up on the cutting room floor, or at least unused in some corner of a hard drive.

Too many times you'll see gorgeous panning shots that slowly, slowly move across the beautiful landscape and seem to go on forever. You'll see zooms that are too slow, or too fast, or shots that are just too short to be useful. That long, slow push into the church steeple becomes an anchor that weighs down the tempo of the story. That perfectly smooth, elegant pan across the skyscrapers of the city drags the video slowly to a stop. What is the viewer looking at when he or she watches this type of slow movement? They're staring at the edge of the screen, watching to see what will next to come into view. It isn't only slow movements that will destroy a scene. Shots that are too short, without enough run-up and run-out will become difficult to edit, forcing the editor to do tricks like slowing them down slightly. Not only are length and pace of the shots important, but poor camera placement, poor composition, and poor staging of the scenes will destroy a video beyond even the capabilities of the greatest editor to reconstruct.

Handling the Camera

The simple fact is that modern digital video cameras are incredible designs of electronic engineering, combining high-quality optics, microscopic digital circuitry, and mechanical precision in an extraordinarily small package. The small size of modern consumer cameras comes at a price. The price is delicacy. They are easy to break from being mishandled, react badly to any moisture, and can easily be damaged by dust and dirt. These cameras should at all times be considered fragile. It's essential that they always be handled with care and treated properly. There are some simple rules to handling DV cameras properly.

First, always hold your camera with two hands. Do not swing them around with the carrying strap, or dangle them from your wrist, or even just carry them loosely with the handle. Any sudden jarring or banging into any hard object can easily damage the camera's tiny circuitry. If you're going to transport it any distance, always put it into a professional camera bag (Figure 4.1). The camera should be taken out only when it's ready to be used.

Figure 4.1 Camera bag

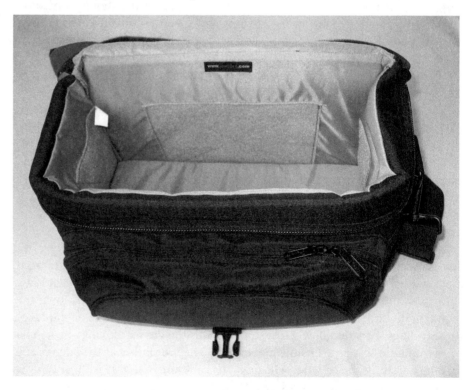

Figure 4.2 Handycam lens

Second, use the camera only when the conditions are right. By that I mean, make sure the camera is under cover, shielded from rain and direct sunlight. Do not leave the camera sitting around to heat up in the sun, or on the dashboard of your car, or even in the glove box of a hot car. Don't leave the camera outdoors for extended periods in freezing temperatures. Also, be careful with sudden changes in temperature, such as going from a warm room or car to a cold exterior, or vice versa. Condensation will not only fog up the lens, but moisture on the tape path and the highly polished metal heads will stop the camera from working.

Third, the camera should always be treated gently. The door should be opened properly, the tape inserted carefully and smoothly, and the door closed again by putting pressure on the correct place, a point usually indicated on the camera. The tape compartment door should never be closed by being slapped shut.

Fourth, the lens cap should be put on when the camera is not in use. On small cameras lenses are amazing small, considering the optical range they support (Figure 4.2). On such a tiny lens any small bit of dirt or dust or hair will be hugely magnified on the screen. You should never touch the lens with your finger. In addition to marring your picture, skin oils will damage the lens coating. Only proper lens tissue or cloth and lens cleaner should ever come in contact with the camera lens. Most consumer camera lenses are not glass but hard plastic and can easily be marred by a nick or a scratch.

Camera Basics

Video cameras work basically by focusing light through a lens onto a chip or a prism that splits the light into its three components—red, green, and blue—and sends each stream to a separate chip. This is the basic difference between a one chip and a three-chip camera. A three-chip camera will always produce better results, and have greater color definition, clarity, and resolution, but it will also be more expensive.

The chip or chips are charge coupled devices (CCDs), the faces of which are covered with thousands of pixels (picture elements). The pixels on a single-chip camera are grouped into clusters that respond differently to red, green, and blue light. On a three-chip camera, all the pixels on the red chip respond to however much red light is falling on the scene and where it appears in the image. Combining these red, green, and blue values will produce all the shades in between, yellow, cyan, and magenta, and all the shades in between those.

These chips respond to the light falling on them and produce tiny electrical currents that are amplified and fed into a buffer. The buffer breaks the continuous electrical stream down into a specific frame rate, emptying about once every 60th of a second. Each time the buffer empties, one *field*—not frame—of video is produced. The North American standard definition television uses 525 horizontal lines in the analog display of a frame, but each field does not contain all the information for that display. It contains only half the number of lines, either all the even-numbered lines or all the odd-numbered lines. The two fields make up a single frame of 525 lines of video. Because the buffer doesn't produce all the lines of a frame at once, but only half of the lines, the image is said to be interlaced. And because an object may be in motion, the two fields in a single frame may not be identical.

Though the analog signal uses 525 lines, some of those lines are used for transmission and timing control. This extra portion of the analog signal, not seen on the television set, is not needed for digital video, which only uses 486 lines. The DV format most widely used in school reduces that further to 480 horizontal lines.

Though television produces images approximately every 60th of a second, the true frame rate for American television is not 30 frames per second but 29.97 frames per second, so each field is actually generated every 59.94 times a second, rather than exactly 60 times a second.

Learn the Controls

Every camera is a little different, yet they all have some things in common: an on/off switch, stop/start button, zoom control, tape compartment, and battery mount. Learn the controls on your camera.

Start of course with how to connect the rechargeable battery to the camera and how to remove it. Without the battery none of the camera controls will function. Usually each camera, or at least each manufacturer, will use a specific type of battery that will mount only on their cameras and only in one way. The battery usually slips into a groove and clicks into place. Make sure it's firmly and correctly seated. There is normally a slide, or button near the battery that releases it and lets you remove it for recharging. Some cameras, unfortunately, have to have the battery mounted to recharge. Usually these manufacturers also make a charger accessory that lets you charge one or more batteries away from the camera. If your camera does not come with a separate battery charger, it's well worth the investment to get one or more of them.

Whenever you go out to shoot make sure you are going with a full battery and with extra batteries. You can never have too many tapes or too many batteries. Always take more than you think you'll need.

Next, learn how to turn the camera on and off. On some cameras, this is a simple two-position switch, but on many cameras this switch can have multiple positions, Off, Camera On, VCR On, and sometimes Still Shot for taking still images. Make sure you've switched it into the mode you want to use. Many cameras also have an automatic switch-off function if the camera is running on batteries and there is no activity, such as starting, stopping, or zooming. Usually the camera will power down in five to six minutes. Some cameras will also have a standby mode, in which the camera will use minimal power but still leave the tape heads engaged for quick start-up.

You should also learn how to connect and power up the camera with a power supply or AC/DC converter, which is normally supplied with the camera (Figure 4.3). Some cameras use a plate that mimics a battery to connect to the power supply, while others simply have a separate power port on the camera body into which the power supply is inserted. Be especially careful when plugging into the AC power that the plug is aligned in the correct manner and that it is firmly pushed into the socket. When the camera is connected to a power supply always be aware of the wire connecting you to the wall, especially if it is connected with an extension cord. If the camera is well away from the power socket, it is always a good idea to tape down the extension cable to help prevent people tripping over the line.

There is usually a release that will open the tape compartment. On some cameras this might take a moment or two while the mechanism pulls itself out from the body of the camera. Make sure you insert the tape correctly in the proper alignment. Then close the door carefully. On many cameras this will often require you

Figure 4.3 Camera power supply

Figure 4.4 Camera tape compartment

to close an inner door first and wait for the mechanism to engage and ingest the tape before you can close the outer door (Figure 4.4).

The Stop/Start button is usually the most noticeable button on the camera. Press to start and press to stop. When the camera is recording there is usually an indicator in the viewfinder or view screen that shows the camera is in record mode. Whenever you start recording make sure this indicator is on. Too often you'll find tapes that have been shot of floors or walls, or close shots of grass, taken by people who were recording when they thought they weren't. Also, people sometimes aren't recording when they think they are. Whenever you put the camera into record mode count down from four before the action begins, and while you're counting down check the view screen to make sure you're recording.

On most camcorders, when you're holding the camera properly a rocker switch for the zoom control falls easily to hand. Learn how the zoom controls work, which way to press the rocker switch to zoom, and which way to press it to zoom out. If the switch is mounted at 90 degrees of the zoom axis, which it often is, the direction of the zoom may be counterintuitive.

Three Important Functions

On every camcorder, there are three functions that need to be changed from the factory default setting. These are usually in the camera menus. Every model of camera will access the menus differently and will have different capabilities in the menu, but some are universal.

The first function to be set is the camera clock. This usually requires that you put into the camera a small lithium ion battery. Check the manual to find out where this is concealed. The battery lasts about a year, and one of its primary functions is to keep the camera clock running. In the menus there will be a function that will let you set the date and time. It doesn't have to be right but it does need to be set. This date and time stamp is recorded on the tape, hidden on a separate information track, which can be accessed by non-linear editing systems, giving them information about exactly when the camera was started and stopped. Make sure the clock is set.

The second item that needs to be changed from the factory setting is the audio sampling rate. All consumer cameras set this to 12-bit, which records the audio at a sampling rate of 32kHz, which is 32,000 samples per second. Using this sampling rate you have access to a feature that allows overdubbing in the camera. But this is a completely unnecessary feature to anyone with access to an editing system, where a great many audio tracks can be added without problem. Rather you should always use the 16-bit setting, which will record the audio at a sampling rate of 48kHz. This will give you two channels of excellent quality audio. You should always switch your camera from 12-bit to 16-bit and leave it there.

The third menu item that you should change is the digital zoom. You should switch it off and leave it off as explained in the sidebar on digital zoom.

What Is Digital Zoom?

Most cameras today tout their ability to zoom 100x or even 500x. Ignore all this. It is a marketing fabrication. Cameras have two types of zoom: optical zoom and digital zoom. The optical zoom is all you should consider when looking to purchase a camera. This is an indication of how far the lens can zoom from its widest to its most telephoto. 16x means the widest angle image will show a picture that is 16 times greater than the most telephoto end of the zoom. This zoom function is changed entirely with the optical characteristics of the lens itself.

What digital zooms do is to go from that optically telephotoed image and enhance the picture by digitally blowing it up. It takes the pixels the digital software creates and makes them bigger. You are no longer zooming; the camera software is simply increasing the size of pixels on the screen by scaling them. The more you blow up the size of the pixels, the softer, blockier, and more mosaic-looking the image will become.

There is never a smooth transition from the optical zoom to the digital zoom, but a slight hesitation as you make the transition from one to the other. Generally, it is always best to switch off the digital zoom function and rely solely on the optical zoom function. This is usually done inside a menu setting. If you really do have to use the digital zoom, you can always turn it on again, but do try to use it only when absolutely necessary and remember to switch it back off when you're finished.

Menu Functions

You should look through the menus to see what other controls you have, such as image stabilization, wind noise reduction, widescreen mode, and many others. The camera may also probably have special effects controls, like posterizing, or black and white, or sepia. I would recommend that you leave these off. Once you shoot with them, in sepia for instance, your material will be in sepia and there will be no way to undo that. If you do want to make your video sepia or black-and-white, any non-linear editor will give you filters that will let you change the material, non-destructively, without altering the original. But if you know you want your whole video to be black-and-white, you can shoot it that way, saving you from having to change it in editing. But once it's made black-and-white this way, it will always be black-and-white.

Many cameras have a widescreen or 16:9 mode. How this is implemented varies greatly from camera to camera. In some instances widescreen mode simply cuts off an area at the top and bottom of the screen, replacing it with black bars. This is called letterboxing and is not true widescreen. A true widescreen mode will shoot in such a way to squeeze the image horizontally, making what's called an anamorphic image that fits into the regular 4:3 image size. When the video is played back it will be anamorphically stretched back to its widescreen aspect and you will see the image correctly. This widescreen image can be seen properly only on a widescreen TV or one that can switch between normal 4:3 and 16:9 widescreen. This widescreen format is appealing in appearance and is widely adopted in much of the world, in Japan, Australia, and Europe in particular but has been relatively slow in gaining acceptance in the United States. You should be aware that material shot in true widescreen should really be used only when you can display your material on a widescreen monitor. You can if you wish, in most editing software, shoot and edit your material in 16:9 and then convert it to 4:3 letterboxed for display on the 4:3 television. This may take a good deal of rendering however.

Using the Zoom

An important feature of most video cameras is the ability to zoom in on a subject. This ability allows you to effectively have a camera with a variety of focal length lenses. What that means is that you have built into the camera a lens that's fairly wide-angle, a normal lens, as well as a lens that moderately telephoto, and everything in between. The zoom of course lets you change the focal length from wide to telephoto and back again while you're shooting, but just because there is a zoom lens it doesn't mean you have to zoom it on every shot. Many movies are made without using zoom lenses or without the camera zooming at all. Use zooming only when necessary. This is especially true for small consumer camcorders, which never have power rocker switches. What this means in practice is that the zoom control has two speeds, go, and go a bit faster. It means that it is almost impossible to smoothly begin a zoom or to end it. Nor can you zoom in quickly, nor, more importantly, can you zoom in slowly, creeping in almost imperceptibly. This is a feature of expensive, professional cameras and is impossible to duplicate on a camcorder. On these cameras it's also sometimes possible to disengage the servo mechanism that drives the zoom and manually zoom in very quickly. This is an important feature for speed in focusing, as we shall see later in this chapter.

Set up a shot and practice shooting, seeing how wide a wide-angle shot is and how telephoto the end of the telephoto is. When you are using the telephoto end of the zoom it becomes ever more important to use a tripod to stabilize the camera. One problem with many consumer cameras is that the wide-angle end of the zoom range is just not very wide-angle and is more like a normal lens. This is done to create a greater telephoto range but at the sacrifice of a useable wide-angle lens. For these cameras, purchase a wide-angle adapter that can be fitted to the front of the lens, giving it a better wide-angle capability.

Use a Tripod

You should work with the camera mounted on a tripod whenever possible (Figure 4.5). The camera should be hand-held only for specific types of shots or if the position of the camera prevents a tripod from being used. In many instances a good substitute is specially designed beanbag that cradles the camera and holds it still. This is especially useful for static shots and lets you use tables or chairs or benches or car hoods or steps as places to steady your camera.

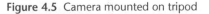

Figure 4.5 Camera mounted on tripod

Tripods can be adjusted in height, either by extending the legs or by raising and lowering a central post. Extending the legs should be your first option, as it will give more stability. The central post should be used primarily for fine-tuning the height of the camera. Better tripods will have a bubble for leveling the camera to make sure it's aligned with the horizon. Use this to make sure the camera is straight. Generally it's a good idea to adjust the height and level of the tripod to the desired position before putting on the camera. Then you can the central post, raising and lowering it as needed to get the lens exactly where you want it.

Learn how to mount and unmount your camera from the tripod. There is usually a separate plate that is removed from the tripod and screwed into the base of the camera. This is often a two-stage tightening system. First you attach the plate to the camera, twisting it a few turns to secure the plate loosely to the camera, and then you use the second screw, which tightens the plate against the camera body. If you have one of these two-stage tripod plates, do not screw the plate completely into the camera in the first stage. This will sometimes drive the screw into body too deeply and crack the circuit boards inside. Also, do not screw the plate into the camera so tightly that you need a power screwdriver or a wrench to take it off. The tripod plate is not a permanent attachment to the camera. The plate should be screwed on tight enough so that it holds the camera steady but loosely enough so that it can be readily removed without tools. Make sure when you put the tripod mount onto the base of the camera that it connected in the correct orientation. Do not screw the camera onto the tripod by spinning it around the tripod plate. Usually you end up screwing it in too tightly and with the camera pointing in the wrong direction. Some tripod plates have an arrow etched on them pointing which way the lens should face. With the plate on the camera, it can be snapped into place on the tripod mount. Usually the plate will have only one direction in which it will mount. On some tripods it can mount in a couple of different directions. Generally you want to put the plate on so the camera lens is pointing in one direction and the tripod pan handle is pointing in the opposite direction. Whenever you put the camera on a tripod, grab it and rock it gently to test the connection to make sure the camera is securely attached to the tripod.

The plate is part of the tripod assembly and should always be removed from the base of the camera after use and reattached to the tripod. Do not leave the tripod plate screwed onto the camera. The next person who wants to use the tripod will not have the plate, and the tripod will be effectively useless without it.

Automatic Controls

Every video camera comes with some functions that are automated. On most consumer or prosumer camcorders (cameras that are the size of consumer cameras but which have some of the features of professional cameras) these functions are all switched on in their automatic mode when the camera is started up. Most of these cameras have a selector switch that will let you switch the camera to fully automatic with a single click. Generally you want to avoid using full automatic mode. You will get a decent image about half the time you're shooting. The rest of the time, the automatic controls will get you in trouble and produce undesirable effects.

The problem with the auto controls is that they're always changing, always trying to adapt to changes in the shot. The changes are often noticeable, and once you've noticed them, you'll see them all the time in material that's shot on automatic.

There are three main auto functions that you usually want to switch off when you're working with your camera. They are:

- Focus
- Exposure
- White balance

Remember that all of these functions, particularly auto iris and auto focus, use battery power, as they are constantly adjusting using the servo drive mechanisms of the camera. Using these functions will shorten your battery life, meaning you'll need extra batteries and have to change batteries more often.

Focus

The main issue with auto focus is that it is continuously trying to adapt to find the focal plane for the object in the center of the screen. The problem is that the subject of interest may not be set in the center of the screen. It often is offset to left or right. The camera may then try to switch between the centered background and the object, repeatedly doing so, constantly changing the focus. This is less of a problem outdoors, on a brightly lit day, where the depth of field (see sidebar) can be very large, from very close to the lens to infinity. Indoors however, or whenever shooting with less light, this can be a major problem.

The problem is that unless conditions are ideal the focus will always be changing, continuously trying to adjust and readjust the focus, creating the effect of the focus breathing as it goes in and out. This becomes especially noticeable indoors or on overcast days when light levels are low. The smaller the depth of field the more critical focus becomes and the more difficult it becomes for the camera to maintain it correctly.

Another problem that occurs with depth of field is when something passes between you and the subject you're shooting. Take the case of a shot of someone across the street. The focus is set on the person, the shot nicely framed, zoomed in to a good telephoto to see them clearly. A truck comes down the street passing

What Is Depth of Field?

Depth of field is the area that's in focus around a subject. When an object is in exact focus, there will be an area in front of it that is in focus and an area behind it in focus. In the total depth of field, one-third of the distance will be in front of the subject and two-thirds behind the subject (Figure 4.6). There is twice as much depth of field behind the subject than in front of it. How large this area is depends on three primary factors:

- The size of the field of view
- Distance to the subject
- Amount of light getting into the lens

On a wide-angle setting, or with a wide-angle lens, the depth of field will appear to be great. However, the more you zoom in the smaller the depth of field gets. Outdoors on a bright day, the depth of field, even with a telephoto lens, might be quite large, but as the light level reduces, especially indoors, the depth of field can fall dramatically. The closer the subject is to the lens, the smaller the depth of field becomes. A close shot of a small object indoors can produce a depth of field that will be no more than a couple of inches, a small window to get the object in focus.

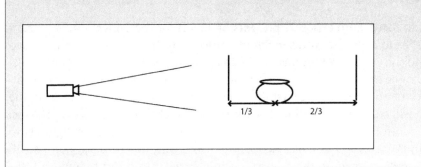

Figure 4.6 Depth of field

between the camera and the subject. Normally this would just be a momentary blur, which could enhance the scene, but with auto focus on what will happen will be that the focus will change to the truck, and then when the truck is gone, your subject on the far side of the street will momentarily be out of focus, until the auto focus adjusts itself again. This constant changing of focus gets annoying and is unpleasant to watch. It is unacceptable in professional video and should be unacceptable to you. So how do you avoid this problem? The answer is pretty simple: Set the focus manually, or at least set the focus and then switch off the auto focus.

Another reason depth of field is important is its ability to isolate an element in a shot. The eye follows what's in focus. If the foreground is in focus and the background soft and blurry, the audience's eyes are riveted to the foreground subject. Conversely if the foreground is out of focus the audience will concentrate on what's in the background. Directors often use this as a powerful tool, changing the focus during a shot from a foreground subject to something or someone else in the background. Changing the focus like this is called a rack focus or to rack focus. Being able to rack focus is possible only if the depth of field in the image is small enough to show enough distinction between foreground and background.

Setting the Focus

The key to setting focus properly is to do it when the camera is zoomed in as far as it will go. This will give you the tightest depth of field and the most precise focus. If you try to focus when you are not fully on telephoto, the focus may be close, but the depth of field might make you think you're in focus when you're actually not. The chances of getting this right are slim. If you then zoom in you'll probably find that the focal point has not been set correctly. So always set the focus when zoomed right into the subject as far as the optical zoom of the lens will allow. Once you're zoomed in, set the focus manually, or with the camera on auto focus, let the camera set the focus with the subject centered. Once the focus has been set, switch off the auto focus function. There is usually a slider switch or button that will do this. Now you can zoom back out, reframe the image however you like, and the focal plane that you set will remain. When the truck passes between you and the subject it will pass by as an out of focus blur and the camera and audience will remain focused on your subject on the other side of the street.

Exposure

Like auto focus, auto exposure presents problems for the camera under all conditions. Auto exposure works much like auto focus. It's constantly changing to adjust to the current conditions. As the image changes so will the exposure. Take our example of the street scene above. If the truck that passes between the camera and the subject is a large, white and very bright truck, the exposure on the camera will change to accommodate the sudden brightness of the scene. The iris, which controls exposure in the camera, will close down, letting less light get to the lens. When the truck has passed, the scene will now be dark, the iris will slowly open up again to the original setting. As with auto focus, you'll get this momentarily bad picture, not only out of focus, but dark and out of focus, before they adjust to the subject again.

If you had the camera on manual exposure the truck might be overly bright as it goes by, but the scene would still be correctly exposed for your subject, which is what you want. It doesn't take objects as large as trucks to affect the exposure; even small changes will impact the exposure. If you are taking a picture of someone wearing a white shirt and they change position so more of the shirt is seen, the auto exposure function will change the iris setting. This means the setting for the person's face will get darker. As they move about the exposure will constantly adjust to the brightest object and the amount of brightness in the scene, which means that the subject's face will be constantly getting darker and lighter. This is as unacceptable as poorly changing focus.

The same thing can happen when shooting against a bright sky, especially on an overcast day. On a sunny day there is a lot of light falling on the subject and the sky is usually blue, so it is not so bright; there's less of difference between the subject and the background sky. On an overcast day however, there is less light falling on the subject while the sky is often almost white. Now there is a large difference between the amount of light on the subject and the white background sky. In this kind of scene, the exposure will be constantly changing depending on how much sky is visible in the shot. Zoomed in tightly, getting a close shot of the subject, with little sky, you'll will probably get good exposure for the face. As you zoom out or change to a wider shot, the exposure will change, the iris will close down again, and the subject will immediately turn into a silhouette, or at least become much darker than in the closer shot, probably so dark that you won't be able to see any facial detail or expression. The correct way to shoot this is to use an intermediate setting, one that's acceptable for a close shot and will not be too bright on the wider shots. And the only way to do this is to switch off the auto exposure function.

Setting the Exposure

Just as in setting the focus, the key to setting the exposure is to do it when you're fully zoomed in, or at least zoomed in to your optimal framing to what looks correctly exposed in your viewfinder. Zoomed in like this, let the camera find its correct exposure, and then switch off the auto exposure function. Again this is usually done with a slider or button. Once auto exposure is off, your setting is locked, and it will not change as you zoom in or out or reframe the shot, or if the content of the scene changes, as when the white truck drives by.

White Balance

Our eyes see the world as if all light was the same—sunlight, overcast, neon light, indoor tungsten light. Our brain adapts and compensates for the differences in light. Cameras however have no such intelligence. They have to be told what color the light is, and the color of light varies enormously. The light source will often be predominantly more one color than another. This is what the white balance control adjusts.

Exposure Controls

Cameras will have different exposure controls. Some will be simplified, a basic indicator in the view screen showing you a bar that displays the range of exposure settings and your current position. Others will include f-stop numbers. These are values for the amount of the iris opening. The higher the number the more the iris is closed, the less light will get to the camera, and the darker the image will be. On a bright day the f-stop can be f-16 or f-22. The lower the number the more open the iris is and the more light that is allowed into the camera. Indoors the f-stop will typically be f-5.6 or less.

Figure 4.7 Zebra

Some cameras, especially prosumer cameras, will have what's called zebra (Figure 4.7). Zebra are diagonal stripes that appears in the viewfinder to indicate when the exposure reaches a certain level. The level at which zebra appear can be changed in some cameras. The most common setting is 75 percent luminance. With this setting, bright highlights on a person's face might show a little zebra marking. If the face is fully zebraed, the scene is overexposed and washed out. If there is no zebra in the shot, even when there is a bright sky, or on a white shirt, then the shot is badly underexposed. For most scenes the brightest areas of the shot will show some zebra, without too much intruding on the subject. Sometimes zebra is set to 100 percent, and then it's used to indicate the peak level that should not be exceeded. If zebra is available on your camera it's an excellent tool you should learn to take advantage of.

The color of light is measured in degrees of Kelvin, a temperature-measuring system based on absolute zero. As you heat a block of carbon it changes color. At 3,200 degrees Kelvin, the carbon produces light that is quite yellow. This is comparable to indoor tungsten lighting. At 5,600 Kelvin the carbon will produce a bluish light, which is comparable to daylight on a sunny day.

On most cameras there are four settings for white balance:

- Automatic
- Daylight
- Tungsten light
- Manual

The daylight setting, usually indicated with a sunburst symbol, tells the camera that the light falling on the scene is the equivalent of 5,600 Kelvin, though on a day with heavy cloud it may be as low as 4,500 Kelvin. The camera fixes the light setting for that color of the light source. The tungsten setting, usually indicated with a light bulb symbol, tells the camera the light source is indoor lighting, which has a color temperature of 3,200 Kelvin. The automatic setting changes constantly, adjusting to the scene, balancing for the content. The problem with the automatic function is that it can be influenced by the content of the scene. If someone is wearing a bright blue shirt, the camera will tend to overcompensate and will often produce skin tones that are too warm and orange.

One problem with automatic systems is that they are slow to react to sudden changes, for instance when taking the camera from indoor lighting to the outdoors. It may take the camera up to a minute before it changes its white balance to adjust to the new lighting. Another problem might be shooting late in the afternoon or at sunset. You may want the warm light of that time of day. As sunset approaches, the color temperature will get lower and lower, warmer and more yellow. If the camera is on automatic it will continuously adjust to remove the warmth of the light, the opposite of what you might be trying to achieve. In this instance, it's probably best to leave the camera set for daylight and let the natural warmth of the light affect the image.

Fluorescent, sodium, and mercury vapor lighting will often present major problems for white-balance systems. The latter two in particular present problems because they actually omit portions of the color spectrum, making reproducing true color in video almost impossible. Older fluorescent lights often are in the greenish portion of the spectrum; they also tend to change over time. In these instances it is particularly important to set the white balance manually.

Setting the White Balance

In most instances you're probably best served by using one of the presets, either the tungsten setting for indoors, or the daylight setting for outdoors. In circumstances where there is mixed light, for instance indoors with window light or outdoors if the light is unusually filtered through cloud or smog, then the white balance

---

This is a classroom exercise to familiarize yourself with the controls on your camera.   *Exercise: Camera Controls*

1 Divide the class according to the number of cameras and tripods available. Ideally there should be no more than four students to a camera.

2 Each of the students in each group should practice setting up the tripod, mounting the camera on it, and attaching the battery or power supply.

3 Look at turning the equipment on and controlling the various functions. See how the zoom operates, how to set the menus, how to focus, set the exposure and the white balance.

4 Learn how to take down the equipment, how to collapse the tripod and how to put away the camera for proper storage.

should be set manually. This is relatively easy to do. As when controlling other automatic functions, this is best done when zoomed in very close. In this case you should zoom into a white card, or white sheet of paper, or white T-shirt, leave the camera on automatic white balance, or depending on the camera controls press a white-balance activation button and let the camera adjust itself to the color of light falling on the white object. What you're doing is telling the camera that this is what should look white. Once the camera has adjusted to the light, either switch off the auto white balance, or release the white-balance activation button.

5

Shots and Angles

The camera is the tool that you use to interpret the scene you're shooting. It's a way of showing the scene, but more importantly it's a way of selecting pieces of the scene to show and to emphasize. Whenever you decide to shoot a scene in a certain way, point the camera wide or tight, you are deciding what your audience should see; you're selecting and emphasizing aspects of the scene for your audience to view.

Most scenes begin with an establishing shot. This is usually a wide shot that shows the whole scene and the setting. From here the camera progresses to closer shots to point out specific things to your audience. It's important to understand what effect shooting a scene in a specific way will have on your audience. If you want to create a specific effect in your audience it's important to know what shots you need to shoot and how you need to shoot them to create the response you want.

The camera's zoom lens lets you set a variety of different lens settings, starting from a wide angle that gives a field of view of about 45 degrees. That's wide for a camera, but not very wide compared to our field of view, which with our peripheral vision, can see to about 120 degrees. You can make a lens that shows this great field of view or even more. Like your eye, the camera lens is a spherical lens. The problem is that your eye has a brain behind it, while the camera does not. Your brain is able to take this round image of the world and change the inherent distortion in it, take the vertical lines that are bent into curves and straighten them out so they appear as we normally see. This kind of very wide-angle lens, called a fisheye lens, does not have a brain behind it, and the lens will produce an incredibly distorted image. All the vertical lines will appear curved, and the image will bulge in the middle and bend away at the edges.

When the camera is on its telephoto end of the zoom the field of view may be around 5 degrees, a very narrow angle, like looking down a tube. There is distortion in this type of lens as well, apparent compression of distance, and flattening of curved surfaces.

Every lens, except when in its normal setting, the equivalent of 55mm in still cameras, will produce distortion in the image to some degree or other. The more extreme the lens the greater the distortion. Photographers and directors use these distortions of the camera lens to help them emphasize some things, to diminish other things, to create an effect of speed, or of slowing down, make someone seem important or inconsequential.

Wide Angle

Wide-angle lenses have characteristics that affect the image they produce (Figure 5.1). A wide-angle lens will create the appearance of objects being far apart, as if there is great separation between them. You should try this out for yourself by lining up two objects, one behind the other separated by a yard or so. With the wide-angle end of the zoom, the two objects will actually appear quite far apart, much farther apart than the few feet between them.

There are some other obvious examples. If the lens is pointed down a street, it will appear as if it were wide and long, broad in the foreground, tapering quickly to point toward the horizon, creating the impression of great depth. If a car comes

Figure 5.1 Wide-angle shot

down the street toward the camera, it will at first appear very small, and then quickly become very large and rush past the lens. This fast apparent change in size will create the impression of great speed as the car whooshes by. You see this all the time in the coverage of car races.

One problem with many consumer cameras is that, though they provide a good range from wide angle to telephoto, the widest angle is not very wide, often no more than the equivalent of a normal lens in still photography. The lack of a true wide-angle lens on most camcorders makes it advisable to get a wide-angle adapter that fits on the front of the camera lens and allows you to create a true wide-angle shot. This is especially useful for sports and other types of action events.

Telephoto

The telephoto end of your zoom will also change the way the image looks (Figure 5.2). If you take your setup of two objects about a yard apart and shoot it with the telephoto end of your zoom lens, you'll see that the objects appear much closer to each other. The distance between the two is greatly compressed, with little apparent separation between the objects. (To use your telephoto you might have to move farther back from the objects.)

If you looked down the same street as you did before, but now with your telephoto lens, you'll see the street looking much more compressed. It will appear shorter and not as broad. There won't be the same pronounced tapering from wide to narrow at the horizon; the street will appear consistently wide from foreground to background. The car coming down the street toward you will now appear to be

Figure 5.2 Telephoto shot

hardly moving at all. There will be no sensation of speed, and instead of rushing past, it will appear to slowly drift out of one side of the frame as it goes by.

Low Angle

The height of the camera is important in giving the audience a sense of how they should perceive a scene. The distortions of the lens that we've just seen are further emphasized by using the height of the camera. When you watch films you will see that the camera is rarely at normal height; it is almost always either below or above the subject's eyeline, always either looking up or looking down at someone. Directors use the height of the camera to change the audience's view of the subject. Shooting from a low angle, pointing upward toward the subject, will make it seem imposing, dominating and large. Combine that with a wide-angle lens and you get a sense of power and importance. You'll see this in every football game on the sideline camera shots.

High Angle

The high angle, looking down on a subject, produces the opposite effect, diminishing the subject, making it look small, insignificant, or less important. Combine that with a more telephoto lens than normal and you effectively demean the subject, reducing it in the eyes of the audience.

Dutch Angle

Shooting "Dutch" is a special-effects technique in which in the camera is tilted at an angle. You can see this technique often used in music videos, sports, and dramatic movies. The term is has nothing to do with the Dutch but is a corruption of the word "Deutsch," which means German, and was a technique first used in German expressionist movies in the 1930s. Shooting Dutch is unsettling for your audience and should only be done sparingly, but when used properly it can be powerful as it makes the image look dynamic and active. It works well in action and high drama, but when used in other instances it's often laughable.

Rule of Thirds

When you look at a rectangular image like a television, your eyes tend to look at specific areas of the screen. Your eyes do not tend to look at the center of the screen; it fact they spend little time there. Your eyes tend to travel around specific lines of strength within the shape. These lines fall one-third from the top and bottom of the image, and one-third from the left and right side of the image (Figure 5.3). Your eyes tend to drift around these areas of the screen, occasionally moving diagonally from one corner of the central area to the opposite side. This is the rule of thirds: The most important objects in the image, what you want your audience to focus on, are placed on or close to these lines. In the case of a close shot of a person's face, the eyeline is placed not in the center of the screen, but on the top one-

Figure 5.3 Rule of thirds

third line, and if the shot if very close, this will cut off the top of the person's head. That doesn't matter, what matters is that the eyes are correctly positioned. One good thing about this is that if all your shots are framed to match this one-third line then every time there is a shot change the viewer is initially always looking at the same spot on the screen, at the subject's eyes.

It's good to practice using the zoom controls to zoom in and out of a person's face. If you start with the person correctly framed in a close shot, eyes framed on the upper one-third line, and zoom out, the end framing is poor. The subject's head ends up in the center of the frame, moving lower and lower as you zoom out. To keep the subject's eyes and head correctly framed on the one-third line, you have to tilt the camera down as you zoom out. As you zoom out from a close shot, you'll soon see over the top of the subject's head, and after that the position of the head will change less and less, rather you'll reveal more and more of the body as you zoom out. This area above a person's head is called headroom, and you want to keep some but not so much that the shot becomes badly framed, so that head becomes too low in the frame, too close to the center of the screen. Conversely if the camera is correctly framed for a wide shot, a zoom in will have you end up in the middle of the chest. To correctly frame for the end of the zoom, you will have to tilt the camera up as you zoom in. These moves take a little bit of practice to get used to, and it's well worth the effort to learn to be able to do this smoothly.

The rule of thirds applies equally to shooting in widescreen, though the one-third vertical lines are farther apart than in the normal 4:3 screen.

Differences in eyeline position on the screen or sudden changes in headroom between shots can be disturbing to the audience. Sudden jumps in the eyeline or the amount of headroom should be avoided. It's not effective to be used as a dynamic change in the composition, and it's noticeable enough to be annoying.

Safe Action Area

The viewfinders of professional cameras are scribed with marks that indicate what's called the safe action area. As we saw in the previous chapter, the areas on the edges of the frame are cut off by the masking of the television set. If your viewfinder or view screen has no marks that indicate where the safe action area is, be aware of the limits of what's seen on the television screen and allow for it, or mark your view screen in some way so that you have an indication where the real limits of the frame are.

Shots

Though we can see a wide field of view we really don't look at the world in a wide-angle scene. We are continuously looking at specific objects within the scene. We see the street, then we see the red Mustang convertible parked on the other side, then we might see the people sitting in the car. We're looking at a wide shot, then a closer shot, and then an even closer shot. We might notice someone approaching the car; our eyes move, but we really are just changing our view from one object to another. As we look at the clock on the tower at the end of the street, our eyes, even our head, might move, and our eyes "zoom" in, but we don't see the movement. We only register the world in a series of single, usually static shots: car, occupants, person approaching, the clock. Pretty much the only time our eyes can be said to register the movement is when we're following something in motion with our eyes.

This is what the director and the camera operator try to emulate when they're shooting a scene. They try to reproduce the world as we might see it, moving from one object of interest to another. To do this they take a variety of shots of different sizes. These shots have names that you should become familiar with. This is not an exact science. One man's medium close shot might be another woman's medium shot, but this is a general reference to shot sizes.

1   Extreme close-up (XCU): a shot of part of a body, an eye, lips, a shoe, or a ring on a finger (Figure 5.4).

2   Big close-up (BCU) or *60 Minutes* close-up: a tight shot of a person's face, with the eyes on the upper one-third line, the bottom of the frame cutting off below the lips and the top of the frame cutting the person's forehead. Be careful you don't get so close the subject appears to be nibbling on the bottom of the frame. This is an intense close-up used for closely watching someone or in intimate situations (Figure 5.5).

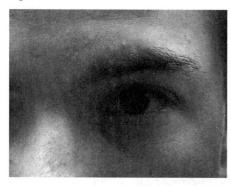

Figure 5.4 XCU

Figure 5.5 BCU

Figure 5.6 CU or CS

3 Close-up or close shot (CU or CS): from just below the neck to just above the head. If the subject has big hair, some of it might get cut off (Figure 5.6).

4 Medium-close shot or bust shot (MCU): a little headroom at the top of the frame, with the bottom of the frame falling in the middle of the chest, just below the bust (Figure 5.7).

Figure 5.7 MCU or bust shot

Figure 5.8 MS

5 Medium shot (MS): about half a person, from about their hips to a little above their head (Figure 5.8).

6 Medium-long shot or three-quarter shot (MLS): from above the subject's head to below their knees, about the middle of the shins. The French call this the American shot, as it was popularized in the American movies in the 20s and 30s (Figure 5.9).

Figure 5.9 MLS or three-quarter shot

Figure 5.10 LS

7 Long shot (LS): any shot that shows the whole subject and some of the surrounding area. This is perhaps the most nebulous shot description in that it can cover a large area. Generally anything from just around the person to any shot wide enough that still clearly holds the subject as the center of interest rather than just another object in the scene would be considered a long shot (Figure 5.10).

8 Wide shot (WS): a general shot of a scene, which may include the subject, placing the subject in context so he or she is another object within the frame (Figure 5.11).

Figure 5.11 Wide shot

Figure 5.12 OTS

9 Over-the-shoulder shot (OTS): a foreground close shot of the back of a person's head with another subject over the foreground shoulder. This is used often in interviews or in intimate scenes (Figure 5.12).

10 Reverse: a second shot after an OTS. It uses the same framing as the first, only the subjects are reversed. The subject over whose shoulder the first shot was taken is now the person framed in the second shot (Figure 5.13).

Figure 5.13 Reverse

Figure 5.14 Two shot

11 Two shot or three shot: typically used to describe a shot in which a small group of two or three people is seen. The framing varies between a medium-close shot and a three-quarter shot (Figure 5.14). If there's more than three it becomes a crowd shot, which is any generalized shot that shows a large group of people. Or it might be a shot that shows the stands in a stadium. Like a long shot, it can vary considerably based on the context.

There are some rules for good framing when shooting pictures of people. It's generally a good idea to avoid shots that exactly cut the subject at their joints. Avoid shots where the bottom of the frame is at the throat, right on the waistline, or cuts people right on the elbows or the knees.

Though these shot sizes are based on human proportions, they are also used as references to other objects. So you might talk in terms of a close shot of a car that shows a headlight, or a medium shot of a house that shows a portion of the building, maybe the lower stories, while a long shot of the same building would show the entire structure.

Camera Movements

The camera is not always static, and one of its great advantages is its ability to move with, into, or around the subject. Make these camera movements as smooth as possible. It's best to do them with a camera mounted on a tripod with a fluid head, or some other type of mount that stabilizes the image. Here are the most typical camera moves:

1 Zoom: going closer or farther from the subject using the optical characteristics of the variable focal length lens, which we have already seen. This is

a completely artificial movement as it's not something that can be reproduced by the human eye or by body movement. A lot of this type of movement, tromboning with the zoom button, constantly going in and out, is the mark of a poor camera operator and the sign of an amateur videographer.

2 Pan: a shot in which the camera is pivoted horizontally around a fixed spot. This is used to follow a moving subject such as a car or someone running. This is panning's most effective use. Generally a movement in the frame that's from left to right is more positive than a movement from right to left, probably because that's the direction in which we read. It's also used to move the audience from one object in the scene to another. It should be used sparingly for this, as the movement tends to slow down the scene. Make the movement follow something or someone who motivates the move, so the camera appears to be following a subject but the camera is really leading the audience from one point of interest to another. If you are going to pan from one subject to another, have a definite starting and ending point. It looks clumsy when you make an edit into an unfinished pan.

3 Tilt: pivoting the camera vertically around a fixed point, such as moving from a person's feet to their face, or vice versa. Like a pan, this shot can slow down the scene, so generally it's best to use it sparingly and for specific effect. Like a pan, it's important that the shot end on a specific point of interest such as a flag or the top of mountain or a skyscraper.

4 Track or dolly: a horizontal movement of the camera, moving either sideways around or following a subject, or moving the camera closer or farther from the subject. Though the term *track* is generic to all these types of movements, usually track is used to refer to a sideways movement, though then it is sometimes referred to as a crab. The term *dolly* is generally used to mean a movement that goes toward the subject or away from the subject, though not all people use the term in that sense. Though the movement can look similar to a zoom, it is quite different and more closely resembles human movement, going closer to a subject or moving away from it. The difference is that in a zoom the plane of the scene does not change, while when tracking into or out of a subject, the plane is continually changing and the perspective of the scene changes around the center of the image. For instance, a tracking shot can also be used to follow a subject as they walk or drive. A shot from one car to another might be called a tracking shot, though if the camera is in or attached to the car that's moving, the shot is not considered a track, but rather a close shot or medium shot of the occupants or perhaps even of part of the vehicle. Tracks are often done hand-held with the cameraperson walking, usually when using a specialized mount such as a Steadicam or a smaller variant to smooth out the motion.

Composition

How a subject is framed on the screen is the composition of the shot. Generally the most important part of the scene is not placed in the center of the frame, but, as we've seen, on the one-third lines that define the Rule of Thirds. Generally when you're taking a shot of someone, the subject is not framed so they are looking directly at camera and almost never in the center of the frame. The exception to this rule is the president of the United States or a news anchor who speaks directly to the audience. Reporters also speak directly to camera, but even they are rarely centered in the shot. All other people never speak directly to camera; they are always looking to either the right or left of the camera. This creates the illusion for the audience that it is simply a voyeur or eavesdropper, an observer looking on at what's happening. It's an illusion we as the audience have come to accept readily, and when this illusion is broken by an actor turning and directly addressing the camera, it is a little disconcerting and unsettling for the viewer as it completely changes the relationship between audience and subject. The audience is no longer the simple observer but now a direct participant.

To maintain this illusion the subject is usually photographed looking slightly to the right or left. Because of this the subject is framed to one side of the screen; if they are looking left, the subject is placed on the right side of the frame, and if they are looking right, then the subject is placed close to the left one-third line. This leaves a certain amount of empty space in front of the subject in the direction in which they're looking. This is called noseroom, and you want to have some of it (Figure 5.15). Otherwise the subject appears to be looking off the edge of the frame and the audience's eyes are drawn over their shoulder to what might be coming up

Figure 5.15 Noseroom

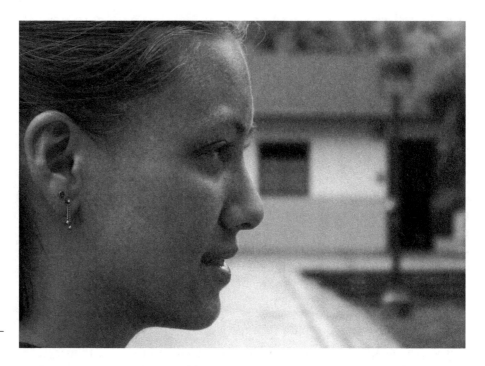

Figure 5.16 *Profile shot*

behind them. This may be useful in suspense and horror movies but not much else. Generally the closer the subject is to looking directly at the camera, if they're looking just to the side of the camera, the closer the subject is moved toward the middle of the frame. As the subject looks farther and farther away from the camera, more into profile, the more the subject is placed toward the edge of the frame and the more noseroom they're given. A close shot of a person in profile does not show the rear of the person's head, which is cut off by the edge of the frame, while in front of the person more of the screen may be empty for noseroom (Figure 5.16).

What About Widescreen?

The rules of framing two people in conversation are often broken when shooting in widescreen. Here you have a couple of simple choices when trying to create an intimate or intense conversation. One choice is to use over-the-shoulder shots that crowd out much of the frame. This works well, but in a movie theater it means that the audience has to do a lot of eye travel, swinging their eyes back and forth as the shot changes between the two people. What's done more often these days is to keep both subjects on the same side of the frame: one person looks left to right, correctly framed on the left side of the screen, often in an over-the-shoulder shot blocking out the right side of the frame, while the other person is also shot on the left side of the frame, looking out the left edge of the frame. This often looks awkward, but it allows viewers to keep watching the same area of the screen and not have to force them to travel their eyes across the width of the screen.

How much noseroom a subject gets is particularly important when the subject is in motion. If someone is walking down the street and the camera is tracking or panning with them, the camera needs to lead the subject, always ahead of
them, keeping them slightly to the side of the frame away from the direction in
which they're moving. A good rule of thumb is that the faster the object is moving, the more the camera should lead them. For a shot of a fast-moving car we
might only see a portion of the vehicle with plenty of space in front of it for the
camera to lead it. This helps to create the illusion of speed, especially if the subject is relatively static in the frame while the background is moving past rapidly.

This is a classroom exercise to practice framing and zooming.

Exercise: Rule of Thirds

1 Set up a classroom monitor with a Rule of Thirds grid. Do this by either
   drawing with a grease pencil on the screen or by putting thin strips of tape
   on the one-third lines.

2 Set up a camera and connect its output to the monitor.

3 Each student in turn should pick a "target," shoot a close shot of a fellow
   student's face and place it correctly framed on the lines of the grid.

4 Each of you should practice zooming in and out while keeping the face
   properly framed on the grid. This will require tilting the camera down as
   you zoom out, and tilting up as you zoom in.

This exercise is excellent practice, and every camera operator does it routinely
whenever he or she sets up a camera on location or in the studio. It helps to get
the feel of how the zoom is performing and how the lens frames the image, how
far in or out you can go before to the image is too big, or before you're shooting too wide, off the stage, or including extraneous objects.

Basic Direction

The framing described above creates an artificial eyeline for the audience, a direction in which the subject is looking, either to camera left or to camera right. This
eyeline direction is the basis for all video and film production. It's the first step in
directing or staging a scene. The director, by placing his camera, creates a relationship between the audience and the subject and also between the subject and other
people or objects in the scene. If you want to show two people talking to each
other, they are facing each other. One is looking to camera left, and the other is
looking to camera right. If you correctly frame the close shots of each of these two
people you will maintain the illusion that they're looking at each other as long as
they continue to face their respective directions. What you're doing is establishing
an imaginary line that runs through the scene, that joins the heads of the two
people in the scene. As long as you keep your camera on one side of that line,

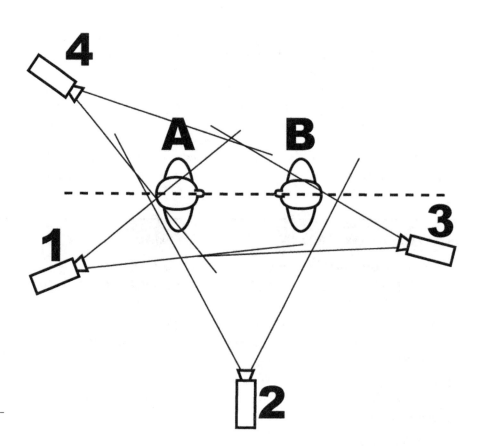

Figure 5.17 The Line

whichever side you choose, the subjects will always maintain the same relationship to each other. This is the basic rule of directing: don't cross The Line. Because this rule is so simple it will always work. The camera can move wherever it wants in an 180-degree arc so long as it stays on the same side of the line (Figure 5.17).

In Figure 5.17 the camera can be placed in positions 1, 2, or 3 and the relationship between A and B will always remain the same. A will be looking from left to right, and B will be looking from right to left. As soon as the camera is placed in position 4, the relationship changes and A and B swap positions on the screen. This can be disconcerting for viewers; their reaction can be that one person has turned his back on the other or that someone is leaving. It marks an abrupt change in the conversation, as if it's over, which may not be what you want.

If you do need to get the camera to the other side of the line, the best way is to do a shot in which the camera tracks around the subject, showing your audience that you're changing their relationship on the screen. This is so important in sports, to get a sense of the relationship and direction of movement, that if the camera has to cross the line a caption is put on the screen, saying something like "Reverse Angle." That may all right for a football game, but obviously it's not something you want to resort to during an intimate conversation.

The rule of the line is important for objects or people in motion. If the bike is moving down the street in one direction, let's say from left to right on the screen, in subsequent shots you want the bike moving in the same direction. If you need to get to the other side of the line, the simplest way is to insert a shot that has the object coming straight toward you or going straight away from you. Then in the next shot you can change to whatever side of the line you prefer without breaking the overall continuity.

When shooting people or objects, think in terms of changing the angle of the shot. As we saw in the previous chapter a small change in the size of an object on the screen creates a jump cut. There are two ways to avoid this. One is to change the size of the shot, not from big close-up to close shot, which would be too small a change, but from big close-up to medium shot, or from close shot to long shot. The second way is to change the angle of the shot. Again a small change of angle is not sufficient. Generally the angle change has to be at least 30 degrees and more like 40 degrees to be effective and avoid the appearance of a jump cut.

These are the most basic rules of camera direction that you should be aware of while you're shooting. You should try to follow these simple rules and break them only for effect, when you have a specific reason, to produce an effect in your audience.

Exercise: Shots Exercise

This is an exercise to practice shot framing and basic direction. It comes in two parts.

Part One:

1 Form groups of two to four students with one camera for each group. If there are fewer cameras make the groups bigger, but it would be best if no group were larger than five.

2 Have the students go out with the cameras and tripods and shoot four shots.
Your instructor should assign the class what four shots you need to take. For instance, the instructor might assign a long shot, medium-close shot, big close–up, and close-up.

3 Each student has to shoot each of the four shots in the order they are assigned. The shots have to be taken of another person or object.

4 Each of you should announce on tape, while the camera's recording, who you are and what shot you're shooting.

5 All of the shots have to be static and held for at least five seconds. You're not allowed to zoom while you're shooting, though you can use the zoom between shots.

After all the groups have taken their shots, the tapes should be brought back to the classroom and critiqued on the basics of exposure, focus, color, composition, and framing.

Part Two:

The same groups should shoot four shots again. This time the four shots have to tell a story, or show a progression of events, such as arriving at school, going to a classroom, or making a phone call.

1 Everyone should work as a team to come up with an idea for your progression of shots. The shots can be any size that works for the scene, but they must be a variety of four different sized, static shots.

2 Because this exercise will not be edited you have to shoot your shots in the order of the action. Try to make the shots cut as closely as you can to match the action. Make sure that you have followed the basic principles of camera direction and have maintained the Line.

Once all the tapes have been shot, they should be viewed in the class and critiqued. The basics should be expected: exposure, focus, and color should all be correct. Check that the shot sizes are appropriate and work for what you're trying to show and that direction flows naturally and the angles of the shots work for the story you're telling.

Anticipate Editing

While you're shooting try to ensure that you have sufficient cover of every scene. This often means including a cover shot, or master shot, that shows the whole scene in one continuous action. This can be used by the editor to establish the scene, during the scene to reestablish the location, or as a fall-back if the cutting gets in trouble.

The traditional formula for entering every scene in Hollywood movies is to begin the scene with a wide, or establishing shot, then move into medium shots, and finally close-ups as the scene intensifies. You'll still see this every day in a lot of movies and TV shows. It's used because it works. That said, there is nothing wrong with beginning with a close-up, some important element in the scene, a broken mirror or a knife on a table. This brings the audience into the immediacy of the scene. Even then you should not work completely in close-ups but pull back to establish the scene for the audience where it is, and who is where in the scene.

With the master shot as cover, the scene should then be broken down into a variety of different shots of different sizes, a mix of close shots, medium shots, and long shots. Television is primarily a medium of close-ups. Because the delivery system is still relatively small, not much bigger than life-size, close shots and medium shots work best. Wider shots that may work on a cinema screen might make the subjects too small on a television set, especially to see expressions or details in the scene. Make sure you include cutaways, shots that don't show the principal action, but to which the editor can cut as a bridge to another shot or another piece of the scene.

To Black or Not to Black?

Timecode breaks on videotape recordings have been the bane of video editors since tape machines were invented. Every digital consumer, prosumer, and professional camera records timecode, and it is important that the timecode be continuous and unbroken. When you start shooting, the timecode will be written to the tape, usually beginning at 00:00:00:00. When you stop and start the camera, it reads the previously recorded timecode and starts writing from the number it reads off the tape. If however, after shooting a scene, you go back and review your material, and then go to shoot some more, if you went past where there is timecode, the camera will start writing new timecode beginning again at zero. Every time this happens there is a break in the timecode, and the tape cannot be captured across this break. You will not be able to capture material within three seconds on either side of the break.

There are a number of ways to ensure that there are no breaks in your DV timecode. The simplest way, which I recommend for beginners and students in particular, is to pre-stripe your tapes: that is, record black and timecode on your tape before you shoot. You can do this in any camera. The simplest way is to just put a lens cap on it or point it at a wall. Now whenever you shoot your tape will have timecode written on it. The camera will then read the timecode and start writing from whatever it reads without any breaks. Pre-striping is not a good idea for professional cameras. Many professional cameras record timecode differently and have to be manually returned to the end of the previously written timecode. If the camera operator doesn't do this you will get discontinuities in the timecode numbers that skip time, which are almost as bad as a timecode break that resets to zero.

Any timecode break is liable to cause a sudden loss of audio video sync when you try to capture across it. So if you do have a tape with timecode breaks in it, one of the simplest ways to get around the problem is to dub the tape. In DV there is no quality issue in this process. The audio and video are copied exactly via the FireWire cable from one machine to another, while the recording deck is generating, new clean, continuous timecode with no breaks. You will however, in most cases, lose the DV start/stop information when you dub the tape.

When you're shooting be sure to start rolling the tape three to five seconds before the action begins; also be sure to leave pad, extra footage after the scene is finished. Again try to leave at least three to five seconds after the action ends before switching off the camera. Just because the shot will only be on the screen for five seconds, doesn't mean that you should only shoot for five. It's easy to cut out material in editing, but it's very hard to add in extra material that isn't there if you need it.

While you're shooting try to maintain continuity of direction and also of clothing, appearance, lighting, and sound. Sudden changes in these can be unintentionally funny. To help with continuity and with editing it's helpful to keep a log while you're shooting; often this is done with the aid of digital still shots of the scene, which can be kept on a laptop with notes about the scene and the shots that were taken.

Exercise: Shooting a Process

This is an exercise to make a short video about a process. It can be something simple like making a peanut butter and jelly sandwich, changing a tire, making a cup of coffee, or connecting a computer system. It's important that it be something simple, and something that can be broken down into steps. The video should be silent, and should be 30 to 45 seconds in length.

1 Working in small groups of three to five you should figure out what you can do for your process.

2 Once the topic has been approved by the instructor, you should make a list of the materials you'll need and, more importantly, of the shots you'll need to demonstrate the process.

3 Shoot the process using a variety of long shots, medium shots, close-ups, and even big close-ups where necessary. Take whatever you need to make the process clear to the viewer. Remember you'll need to contract the time to fit into the project length. To do that you'll need to shoot the process with a variety of different shot sizes and angles so you can cut smoothly without jump cuts.

4 Finally capture your video and edit it in your software, contracting the time to the allocated length and making each step clear to the viewer, so that he or she understands every step of that process.

The exercise and the team will be judged by the instructor and the whole class to see how clearly and correctly the process is shown, how smoothly shot and edited, and with the best use of different shot sizes.

Aesthetics

Some shots look better or are more effective than others. Again there are some simple rules that will help to make better pictures.

Framing is about looking at not only how the subject is positioned in the frame but also at the relationship of objects in the frame and at the edges of the frame to see what's intruding and what's being cut off. You don't want to see a lamppost or tree directly behind your subject, making it look as if it's coming out of the top of their head. You also don't want stray parts of an object just poking into the frame, something that will distract the audience's eyes to some extraneous object or person. Better to reposition the camera to right or left so the tree isn't right behind the subject, or either to tighten or widen the shot so the object on the edge of frame is either completely excluded or more clearly included.

Avoid shooting shots that are symmetrical, whether it's houses, cars, or people. They tend to get boring to look at quickly. Rather than shooting the building straight on, shoot it at an angle from a corner of the building to create perspective.

Avoid shots that are unbalanced, where everything of interest is on one side of the frame. This might work for a conversation where you want to swing your audience's eyes from one side of the screen to the other, but for most objects the shot is more pleasing when something on one side of the frame is balanced with something on the left side. On the other hand if something is isolated in the frame, separated from other objects, like it's in a spotlight, the viewer's eyes are immediately drawn to that object.

How you shoot groups of people is important to how your viewer responds to them. If they're seen separated, standing around or sitting with space between them, it will create a sense of tension within the group. The same group shot close together, standing or sitting near each other, will create a sense of unity and cohesion of purpose.

In the real world people often say to wear darker clothes to make you look slimmer. In television the opposite rule prevails. Dark clothes and dark objects look heavier, while light clothes or brightly lit objects will look lighter.

When shooting objects, try to include something in the frame that will give it scale. A shed by itself can be any size, but with a person standing next to it can look either as big as a home, or as small as a doghouse for a chihuahua.

Despite all the tips and suggestions basically you cannot learn to be a good cameraperson from a book. You can only learn from experience and practice, and can only be really good if you have the natural talent and eye and hands for good composition and good movement.

Project: Symbolic Imagery

This is a two-to-three minute project designed to show off your creativity, imagination, and camera skills. You are to make a video based on a poem, either one of your own choice, one you've written, or one that's assigned to you. The video can contain the spoken words of the poem but no other dialog. It can also have natural sound and music, provided the music is copyright-free or music for which you have copyright clearance.

1   Working in small groups of three to five, find a poem to work with. The words must be suitable for a campus environment and must not be indecent, abusive, vulgar, or offensive in any sexual, racial, cultural, or ethnic context. You might pick a poem from your Language Arts classes, or you might take the lyrics of a song and use them as spoken text. The group should present to the instructor the agreed to poem together with a short, one-paragraph pitch that explains the visual treatment of your project. Your poem and proposed treatment must be approved before the group can move forward to the next step.

2 Next you'll construct a plan for shots you'll need to cover the poem. These can be either symbolic or literal images that can be married with the poem. You are trying to take a literary form and translate it into a visual form.

3 Once the video has been shot, it should be critiqued with the whole class. The critique should be based on the material's technical merits, not on how it will be incorporated into the project. That's the next step.

4 The poem or lyrical narration should be recorded and combined with the video and sound effects elements in your editing application.

5 A simple open title and closing credits should be added.

The audience for your project will be your classmates, and the larger campus community of students, teachers, and administration. Hopefully the productions will also be seen by a wider community at large.

Finally, all the projects will be assessed by the class as a whole. Though you and your project will be evaluated as a team, each individual student will also be evaluated for their contribution and effort in making the production successful.

This project, as all future projects, will be judged first, on technical skill; second, on creativity and imagination; and third, on the teamwork, shown in the group.

Shooting Checklist

This is a checklist of essential items to make sure you have with you when you go out shooting.

- **Tape.** Make sure you have enough of it, and then take an extra one if you can.

- **Battery.** Make sure it's fully charged and take at least one spare if you can.

- **Tripod.** Take one with you even if you don't think you'll be using it. Make sure the tripod has its plate.

- **Microphone.** Take whatever microphones you need and make sure that if they require batteries you have spare batteries for them. Test the audio before leaving for the shoot.

- **Headphones.** Always take headphones to make sure audio is being recorded and to make sure it's useable.

- **Script and Production Notes.** As we'll see in the next chapter, these are critical to your production. Make sure you have them with you whenever you go out to shoot.

On location or on the set there is a checklist to ensure your material is properly shot.

- **White Balance.** Set the white balance first. You will probably need to set this only once for each scene or location. Don't change it unless you need to, as variations in white balance will make skin tones change.

- **Exposure.** Set the exposure for each shot. Try to make the shots within a scene have similar exposure and light values so skin tones and details in light and shadow remain consistent.

- **Focus.** Set the focus for every shot so that you get the optimum depth of field for the shot you intend to take.

- **Framing.** Make sure the framing is correct and correctly composed.

- **Direction.** Make sure the scene is correctly staged and that the angles, movement, and eyelines are correct to ensure good continuity and smooth flow of action.

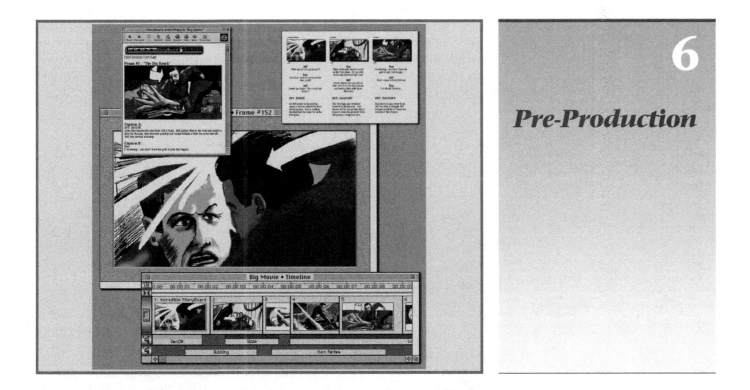

6

Pre-Production

ecause film and video production is based on the notion of time, the process of editing, controlling time and space within the story, is of paramount importance. This process of editing, however, does not begin after the film is shot; it begins when the idea is conceived. As soon as you are thinking of your production as a series of shots or scenes, you are mentally editing the movie, arranging the order of the material, juxtaposing one element against another.

Film and video production is both an art and a craft. In every step, from the writing, to the directing, to the design and photography, to the editing and finishing, every stage is a combination of art and craft. And like every craft it has to be learned. All the other crafts impact the final craft of editing, so it is important that everybody in the production team understands how these crafts interact and impact each other.

Every production begins as an idea. Whether it's a narrative film, a documentary, a music video, an instructional short, a promotional video, or any other form, at some early stage the idea will have to be put down on paper. Until then it is only an idea in your head, and until you can get that idea out of your head onto paper it will forever remain an idea, however good. You may be able to watch your movie in your mind's eye, but of course you'll be the only one. If you want to share your idea, you'll probably first have to share it on paper. Later you may actually be able to share it as a movie. This first step is a huge step and may ultimately affect every step that follows it. I say "may" because the idea as first written down may change considerably and be rewritten into something very different before production even begins and may continue to evolve until it reaches the screen. Nonetheless, this first step can be critical and represents a crucial first point in the production process. This is the point at which the idea should be crystallized in its purest form: what is this movie and what is it about. Because there are such a variety of productions their beginnings may all be quite different. Often the type of production will determine its origin.

■ *Note:* When I use the term *narrative film* I mean movies with fictional stories, the Hollywood and independent feature film being the prime examples. Though many are still shot on real, celluloid film, more and more are video productions, many shot on DV or DVCAM or in high definition. Narrative film, though highly visible as a genre, makes up only a small portion of film and video production in America and around the world. On any single weekend day in June probably more wedding videos are produced in America than all the feature films made in Hollywood in a year, and some of those wedding videos are longer than feature films. Or maybe they just seem that they are.

Many productions are original ideas; many others are commissioned to fulfill a purpose or a need, which in the case of many Hollywood studios is simply to make as much money as possible. Narrative film usually begins as an idea in the head of a writer, producer, director, or occasionally an actor. Sometimes the original writer was a novelist or short story writer, and a producer or studio optioned the original material. Options on books or stories are bought in the hope that they can be developed into a film. An option gives the producer the film or broadcast rights to a story for a specified amount of time, usually a few years. If the producer doesn't pursue the option and purchase the full rights to the material, the rights revert to the original author.

Once the option is taken up and the rights secured, the material is turned over to a writer or team of writers to develop into a treatment.

Brainstorming

At some early stage in the production, especially a collaborative production made by a team of equal partners, you'll have to find ideas about ways to tell your story or get your point across to your audience. This process of fishing for ideas is called brainstorming. Basically it's done by sitting together in a room and coming up with a story or a concept.

How do you start? Where do these ideas come from? First of all, you have to understand that no idea comes fully formed and complete. Ideas grow from other ideas. There are a number of ways to stimulate ideas. Some people use pictures, perhaps of the era, perhaps of a location, or of people. Others like to use toys, simple puzzle toys or dolls or stuffed animals, something that can be engaged kinesthetically. Play is an important part of generating ideas as it lets your mind wander and draw from a lot of different, disparate sources.

There are some rules to brainstorming.

1   There are no bad ideas. Never boo or hiss or put down anyone's idea. No idea needs to be justified or have its origin explained. Do not throw out any idea that comes up.

2   Quantity is quality. This is perhaps the only place where this is true. The more ideas you generate the better you're brainstorming and the more likely you'll be to find good ideas.

3   Make notes. Write down people's ideas. If you don't scribble it down it'll get lost, and finding it again may be impossible.

4   Once everything has been considered, it's time to sort out what you have, to pick and choose, mix and match, and narrow down the field. Bring together ideas that can work together, discard others, and then decide. Don't leave the decision up in the air. Make a decision, even if you have to flip a coin to do it.

Stages of Pre-Production

Whether narrative film or non-narrative film, documentaries, corporate videos, even commercials and music videos, the development of an idea follows remarkably similar lines. First there is a concept, the concept becomes a treatment, which in turn becomes a script.

The Concept: It'll Be Bigger than Titanic

If the basis of the production is not some previous literary work, most productions begin with a concept. The concept becomes a pitch, which is usually a single sheet of paper or perhaps a couple of paragraphs to give the reader a sense of what the project is about. In a narrative film the reader may be a studio executive or a producer. In advertising the reader would be the client, and the pitch would probably be accompanied by displays to show the client how the commercial will look. The pitch for a training video might simply be a statement of what the project is about and how it will be presented. A promotional video might be the description of what will go into the tape, which can range from a simple presentation of a product to complex image animations and musical montages combined with informational content. A music video's pitch might describe the treatment and style given to the song and the performers. A documentary pitch might be a simple description of the reality the production will show.

In addition to a brief synopsis of the project, the pitch will probably include a few sentences or a short paragraph stating why the production is worthwhile, what makes this production unique, why people would want to see it, how it would engage the audience, or why this story must be told.

Think of the pitch as more than just a sales pitch; think of it as your means of defining the production and its goals. This is your concept and your vision.

Always keep your concept bouncing around somewhere in your mind, sometimes right in the forefront, sometimes only at the back of your mind, but always keep it present with you while you're working on a production.

One of the most important points to consider when creating your pitch is to think of your audience. Who do you want to see your production? Is it a broad audience, or a small group of people? What kind of people are they, and how do you communicate to them? Are they affluent teenagers or older middle-class folk? Do they know something about your subject, or will this be completely novel?

Every production has to have a spine, a central theme or idea. This is the concept.

- A grandiose Romeo and Juliet story on an ill-fated liner crossing the Atlantic, as told by the surviving Juliet years later
- How to build and maintain roads in an ecologically sound way on steep, forested land
- The essence of the Japanese artistic style as represented in the work of a great Japanese artist
- The beauty and skill that combine with the violent pain of skateboarding
- The dark and sinister images that define the lyrics, themes, and styles that are at the heart of a rock group's music

These are concepts in their most pared down form. You will want to develop this in a fuller form. The concept is what are you trying to achieve. Will your production be intimate, or vast and sweeping in scope? Is your production going to be sophisticated comedy or slapstick? Will your video be lyrical and romantic, or perhaps hip and edgy? Will your music video be quick, high-contrast, jaggy, hard looking, or will it be soft and airy with slow, fluid movement? Will your documentary be tightly scripted and structured, or will it be loose and free-form, depending on the camera to capture moments? Any producer should quickly see the cost implications of these different types of productions.

By defining the production like this you are setting out your goals. So the concept becomes an important piece of paper. It's what should guide you and everybody who works on the production. This is what we're trying to do. It can be beneficial to revisit this piece of paper many times during the production to ensure that you are still going in the direction you intend. It helps you make sure that you're not going off on a time-wasting tangent, shooting material that you'll never use, or setting up something that does not contribute to developing and enhancing your concept. In documentary production in particular, the material might present itself in a new way as the production continues, or new information might come to light that might change the focus of the story. If this happens it's useful to rewrite the concept. Spend some time reformulating your basic idea of where you're going. Once you've rewritten the concept, keep that as your focus for continued work on the production. Try to avoid rewriting the concept too often. If you find the need to do that more than once or twice in the course of a production, then there is probably something wrong with your work method. Perhaps you aren't doing enough initial research into your subject before you commit yourself to the project.

This idea of maintaining the focus of the production should be important to everybody working on it, especially the producer. More than anyone else it is his or her responsibility to make sure that everyone involved is shooting toward the same target. It is especially important that the producer and the director be on the same wavelength, have the same understanding of the goals, and the same concept of where the production is going and how it's getting there. Get this straight before you begin. The producer and director must work together, or the production is on a long, bad road to trouble, which will dog it from pre-production, through shooting, and on into editing and post-production. If you are the director of photography or a principal actor you need to be aware of the dynamics that are driving the production and prepare yourself for the ride. This is not an issue exclusive to narrative film. This is equally true in documentaries, though there even greater burdens may be put on the camera crew, where conflicting visions can pull in different directions. As the editor you may well have to bear much of the burden of this conflict as well, so if you get involved in a production at an early stage, try to make sure that the principals are acting in concert or at least understand what your position is. Try to stay neutral in what may end as a blow up in your cutting room.

The Treatment: The Three-Act Story

After the concept has been created, the tradition in narrative film is to write a treatment. The treatment is written in narrative form, something like a short story or a novella. It can be anywhere from 10 to 100 pages, though if the producer was presented with a 100-page narrative he'd rightly be concerned that the project might be overly long. This document is essentially a story outline, by tradition written in the present tense, though flashbacks can revert to past tense. The voice is usually that of the narrator, or if the story is from one person's point of view, the hero for instance, then it has that voice. More often than not the voice for the treatment and the movie itself is an omniscient presence. This means that the camera can go anywhere; it can see both what the bad guys are plotting and what the good guys are doing.

The treatment contains the major scenes, the principal characters and their motivations, and the arc of the story. It goes from Act I and the story's premise and the basic conflict, to Act II, the rising conflict, turning point, and the approaching climax, and finally Act III, the climax, resolution, and denouement. This classic structure is used in almost every production to some extent or other, whether it's a documentary, a music video, a promotional video, or even a training video.

For a training video it may be a presentation of what the problem is or the tasks that need to be done, which is Act I. That's followed by showing the viewer how the problem is overcome or the task is done, which is Act II. That's followed by showing how you've accomplished the task, overcome the problem, and reinforcing the objectives in summary form, which is Act III.

A promotional video may begin with the background story of the company or institution and the show the setting and community, Act I; followed by an in-depth look at the facilities, programs, or products, Act II; and finally there might be a summary that emphasizes the greatest of the institution and those in it, and perhaps calls for action on the part of the audience, Act III.

Think of your video project, whatever it is, in this type of structure, and how it best fulfills the story arc. Think of your viewers. They should determine to a huge extent the way your production is framed, the techniques you'll use, and the way you'll tell your story. At some point you will have to engage your viewers on an emotional level, no matter what the production. It's important that you emotionally attract them at the beginning, drawing them into the action by intriguing them, scaring them, stimulating them, flattering them, filling them with awe, showing them beauty or horror, making them tap their feet, or making them want to know what's going on, what's going to happen next, or what's going to come around the corner. If you engage your target viewers at the start of your production you can carry them a long way. It's also important that you leave them with an emotional charge, ending your production so that it essentially makes them want more, makes them want to do something, leaves them either on a high or a low, but leaves them responding on a visceral level. Get the beginning and the end right, and you're more than halfway home. Now you just have to bring them through the middle, and preferably still awake.

Writing the treatment is by far the most fun of the scriptwriting process, before the slog of formatting and structuring the script scene by scene. Even if you were writing a script to develop for yourself, I would not forego the treatment stage. It will help you formulate your ideas, especially the flow and structure of the narrative, keeping to the story arc. Once you're working on the script itself, it's easy to lose sight of the woods from the details of the trees around the scene you're working on. While you're working on the treatment, it's easier to keep the whole forest, meaning the overarching concept of your movie, in the forefront of your mind.

In much documentary work the writing stage often ends with the treatment, which many consider a script. The treatment may be no more than extended production notes, though it's beneficial to advance the written work as far and with as much detail as possible, even to the extent of writing a narration track, which can serve as a guide for the production and where you're intending to go with your material.

The Budget

During the treatment stage you need to consider some important factors about your production and begin to make decisions that will impact that production fundamentally—decisions concerning your budget. You have to consider your location, set design, costuming, talent, props, even makeup. All of these will affect your budget, and your budget may well come to change your treatment as you're forced to find cheaper ways to do what you want.

At some stage fairly early in the production process the budget will have to be created. Whether yours is a Hollywood movie, a student production, or a project in between, you'll have to figure out how much it's going to cost you to make and where the resources to produce it are coming from—if not in terms of hard cash, then in terms of where the costumes are coming from, who's making them, or where the lights or the tape or the extra microphones or that jib arm you want for that opening shot is going to come from.

Budgets are traditionally divided into two parts: above-the-line costs and below-the-line costs. Above-the-line costs are the talent: producer, director, writer, actors, director of photography, production designer, rights fees. These are fixed costs. If additional writers are brought in on a per diem basis, these are part of the below-the-line costs. Below the line is essentially everything else, the services of all the crafts involved plus all the expenses for all the personnel such as construction, lighting, set dressing, props, special effects, post production, mixing, etc. These are all variable costs based on time and union agreements. Most freelancers work at to close to union rates as well. Time is money. The longer it takes to produce your video the more it's going to cost. The more people working on the production the more it will cost. These are the below-the-line elements that you have to weigh: fewer people and slower production versus more people and faster production. Is it more cost-effective to work with one crew and shoot more slowly, or work with multiple cameras and even multiple crews who can leapfrog from location to location? For many narrative films, especially those produced on smaller budgets, it's often more cost-effective to shoot the movie with multiple crews on a short shooting schedule. This requires careful planning and coordination of personnel and equipment but can be productive and a quite enjoyable way to work for many people. It concentrates the effort, focuses everybody, and is often much easier for actors, instead of having the process be drawn out. Think not only of having multiple crews leapfrogging each location, but also think on a smaller scale of shooting scenes with multiple cameras. This is somewhat faster than doing multiple camera setups. The initial lighting may be more difficult and complex, but the speed of completing all the coverage for the scene in a couple of setups is a great benefit. It's also extremely useful when working with inexperienced performers or for interviews. The multiple camera arrangement preserves the spontaneity of the flow of the conversion.

If you need to budget a production, the first step you should take is to get hold of some good budgeting spreadsheets. There are a number of resources for this, such Michael Wiese Productions (www.mwp.com) that have been around for quite a while but that are still useful. What's nice about these budget sheets is not only that they include cost suggestions but that they are thorough in covering of all the little hidden extras you need to account for and often overlook. There are also excellent budgeting and scheduling available from Movie Magic (www.moviemagictechnologies.com). These are invaluable aids.

Sometimes, fairly often in corporate work, there is a budget before there is a concept. A department may have a specific budgeted amount to create a training video. How much does it cost to make the video? There are two basic answers: the first is as much money as you can afford; the second is roughly $1,000 a finished minute. This is a crude guesstimate for most corporate and industrial productions. Again, go carefully through a budget spreadsheet to see what your real costs will be. It's quite possible that in light of budget constraints the concept will have to be revised and a new pitch presented. For corporate work it's not uncommon to prepare multiple conceptualizations and to pitch a few different treatments for a production based on budget considerations, from the quite expensive, to the medium budget video, to the cheap production. One of my favorite sayings in video production is that you can your project can be only two of the following: fast, good, or cheap. It's perhaps a crude representation, but it's a useful axiom to remember.

The Script

After the treatment is approved, the next step is to write the script in screenplay format. For movies this follows a traditional theatrical layout, while for video productions and documentaries in particular, the script layout is based on the tradition of radio plays. If you are seriously interested in writing for the screen I'd recommend you invest in specialist software like Final Draft (www.finaldraft.com). There are basically two formats for scripts: the screenplay format, which is based on theatrical play production (Figure 6.1), and the television or AV script format, which is a development of the format used in radio plays (Figure 6.2).

Figure 6.1 Screenplay format

```
                                                        3.

    4.  EXT.   MOUNTAIN INN - DAWN

        A spectacular sunrise crests the mountains lighting an
        enormous hunting lodge made of huge beams rising in a long
        series of gables, meeting at a giant peak above the vast
        doorway.

                        JAKE(V.O.)
                It was the by chance that I came to the
                inn that morning.

    5.  EXT.   LODGE TERRACE - CONTINUOUS

        ANGELIQUE, a voluptuous 25 year old, is sitting in a deck
        chair, an open LAPTOP propped on her waist. She glances up
        at the WAITER, who leaves a tray with coffee and croissant
        on the table beside her.

                        BELLBOY
                Will that be all, ma'am?

                        ANGELIQUE
                Yes, thank you.

        The WAITER leaves.

        WE SEE:

        The LAPTOP SCREEN as ANGELIQUE types an e-mail message that
        begins "Dear Jake. I'm so sorry it has to end this way."

                        JAKE (O.C.)
                I thought I'd find you here.

        JAKE, a handsome 18 year old, smiles down at ANGELIQUE.

                        JAKE
                What are you writing?

                        ROSALINE
                    (closing the laptop)
                Nothing. Just some e-mail.



                                        (CONTINUED)
```

VISUAL	AUDIO
	MUSIC
	HOST (VOICE OVER)
1 CU looking upstream at a waterfall. PUSH in.	Water...water, the carrier of life...always in motion...home for millions of salmon and steelhead in years past.
2 Stream	Today Coho Salmon are threatened with extinction. Steelhead are also in trouble.
3 Silt in the water	Why? One answer can be found in the water.
4 MS vineyard irrigation	*MUSIC UP AND UNDER*
5 CS water dripping off grapes	Water...the creative force, nourishing life, growth...healing the earth.
6 MCU rivulets running over muddy road	Water, the irresistible force, cleansing, scouring,
7 MCU water pouring down hillside	shaping the face of the earth, sculpting and polishing.
8 MS Damage at Pacifica	Water, the destructive force, eating away at our land, our home...

Figure 6.2 AV format script

In the script or screenplay each scene is fully developed with setting descriptions, dialog, action, and even some camera directions. The tradition is that scripts are written in present tense from the viewpoint of the audience: "We see Jack enter the bar," for instance. Try to work on the premise that the screenplay should describe only what the audience can see and hear and not contain sentences like "Jack thinks about his mother as he listens to Jill." This may be good direction for actors and may be a useful guide for the director, but this is really a form of cheating because obviously your audience cannot see that Jack is thinking about his mother. you want the audience to understand what Jack is thinking, you have to use some technique to show this. It can be simply a series of shots that show his mother, or it can be subtle piece of business, his fingers toying with something that belongs to his mother, or it can be a bit a dialog that refers to his mother. You might write, "Jack fingers his mother's brooch as he listens to Jill." This is now a clue not only to the director and the actor but also to the audience.

The Storyboard

Some productions, commercials, and music videos might skip the script stage and head straight into storyboarding. A storyboard is drawn almost in comic strip fashion, showing the principal shots and setting the style of the production. There is some excellent storyboarding software available such as that from

Figure 6.3 StoryBoard Artist

PowerProductions (www.powerproduction.com). For these types of production the importance of planning and using storyboards for pre-visualization cannot be overemphasized (Figure 6.3).

The great thing about software like StoryBoard Artist is that it gives you so many tools to enhance and detail your storyboard. The StoryBoard Artist software also has the ability to create QuickTime movies of the storyboard material, which is a great tool, particularly for action movies. For complex, expensive productions it also has great value to lay out visually what needs to be done to get good coverage of an expensive scene. There was only one opportunity to burn Atlanta or sink the *Titanic*; here storyboarding is very important.

For smaller productions, this type of pre-visualization may not be necessary. If you have the skills to draw in perspective and to plot out your shots for each scene, storyboarding can be useful. On the other hand if no one of your team has had the training to draw adequately beyond stick figures, your visualization in drawings might be more an expense of time than of real value for your production. What might be more useful in these circumstances is to lay out your script in AV two-column format and use the video side of the script to write in a detailed description of what shots are needed, including size and angle of the appropriate shots. Many productions, such as documentaries, are never storyboarded, and the visualization of the subject is the responsibility of the camera operator.

Your project is to create a PSA that is 60 seconds in length. It should be an announcement or commercial that promotes a school program, club, or team. It may also focus on a teen need or concern, a community organization, or good-will endeavor. What's important is to use your imaginations and the capabilities available to you.

The PSA will be seen by your fellow students and aired as widely as possible.

Project: Public Service Announcement

1 To begin the class will be divided into groups of four or more. The groups should not be too small as there are a lot of jobs to do both in front of the camera and behind it.

2 The group will need to get together and brainstorm ideas for the PSA. Once an idea has been chosen, a concept presentation needs to be prepared. The concepts should be pitched to the class as a whole and must be approved by the instructor.

3 Either a detailed script in two-column format should be prepared, or a detailed, shot-for-shot storyboard should be drawn up. Once the script or storyboard is approved, production can begin.

4 You should use your script or storyboard to guide you while you're shooting. You don't have to follow it slavishly, but stick to your plan and apply the camera techniques you've learned.

5 Do the post-production work, editing, adding transitions, titles, and effects as needed.

The PSAs will first be evaluated by the class, and those that the instructor and class agree should be shown get broadcast and distributed with your available resources.

In this project, and all future projects, the teams will not only be assessed on their technical skill, creativity and imaginative use of camera, sound and editing techniques, but also on their written presentations. The critique will evaluate the quality and professionalism of their initial concept, and the care, thought and writing skills shown in their treatment, scripting and storyboarding.

Delivery

One of the first points to consider in any production is the form in which it will be delivered. This should not be happening when you are in post-production but rather when you are writing and planning your production, when you are shooting, and then finally when you are editing. If your end product is a film to be seen on a large screen, it's shot in a certain way and edited in a certain way. Shots can be held longer because there is so much to see and so much space for the eye to cover and travel around. The same movie seen on the small screen of a television set will appear to be cut too slowly, because you take in the whole image without your eye moving, so you take it in more quickly. Of course, you also see less detail.

If your project is intended for delivery on television, it should be shot for television's limitations of luma and chroma values. If it's shot for delivery on a computer screen, you aren't bound by those limits but perhaps by greater limits dictated by compression. If you're going to squeeze your video down for web delivery, you need to shoot it with as few moves as possible, use few transitions (which don't compress well), and shoot plainer backgrounds. Delivery should be the first consideration in a production, not the last, and every step of the process, from scripting through final editing, should bear the delivery mechanism in mind.

Rehearsals

Rehearsals are important to any production, particularly a drama. These can start out with a dry rehearsal or table read. Sometimes the dialog is changed here to suit the speech patterns of the actors. For costume dramas or any production in which the actors are required to wear clothes they are not familiar with, a dress rehearsal is a good idea. This can be an opportunity to test makeup and lighting and the camera's response to these. Do those colors go well together? Will they stand out against the background or blend in too much? Will more or less lighting be needed to bring out the characters and separate them from the background? As we shall see in the chapter on lighting, little back-lighting would be needed if the costumes are pale and the background dark, while much more would be needed if the costumes are dark against a dark background.

Research

It is hard to imagine that you could do too much research, and this is true no matter what kind of production you're involved in. The more you know about your subject, the costumes of the era, the way people spoke and behaved, the way they dress and wear their hair, the better. Every detail is important to creating a true and meaningful picture for your audience, whether it's for a historical drama or for contemporary production. Some research needs to be done even before the concept is put forward. More research will be needed during the treatment and scripting stage. Research will need to be done by the director, the camera operator, the production designer, the costume designer, and the editor. Everybody has to know the subject from the point of view of the craft they are working in.

As you do your research keep in the mind the focus of your production: what's it about, what's the goal of the production, who's the intended audience. Research can involve many forms of information gathering: using the Internet, the library, looking at pictures, and interviewing people. This can either be done over the phone or on camera. When interviewing someone, always make sure before you begin to write in your notes the name of the person you're interviewing, having them spell their name. Try to ask questions that are open-ended; those are questions that cannot be answered simply with a yes or no. As you do your research make sure you keep copious notes and document the sources of your information.

For corporate productions or promotional videos whether for a company or a school, you will need to research the institution the production is being done for. Is it conservative, old-fashioned, traditional, hip, flashy, edgy, or somewhere in between? You may think you know the institution, but others may have a different view or may be trying to create a different image, to change the way people view the institution or company. You need to understand the background of your subject before you develop your concept. Whether the corporate video is promotional or instructional, you will need to set a tone that matches your client's needs and desires. For promotional videos you will need to explore the institutional style. What other materials are used? For design purposes one place to start is with the color. Every company, club, school, or organization has a color scheme, whether it's in their logo or in their furniture or the color of their walls. Most organizations will have typefaces they use and graphic styles. Be careful, you may have to do some adaptation, as we have seen in the chapter on editing, as the colors, fonts, or styles may not be suitable for video production.

For an instructional video obviously you'll need to understand the process, and you'll need to understand which bits of the process are most critical or difficult. There is nothing worse in an instructional video than belaboring something that to the viewer is obvious, while skipping quickly over something complex or difficult to do or understand. Use your own judgment on this as well as the judgment of the instructors. Some instructors may see something as simple, which to you seems quite difficult. Favor your gut feeling. If it's new to you and looks complex to you, it probably will also be complex to someone else new to the subject. Break down the process into the steps you need to know to do the task. Once you've figured that out you can begin to think about how you will present it to an audience: in a studio, or on location. If on location, which location: a factory floor or a beach on Maui, if only you would be so lucky. Once you've decided on how you'll show the process, you can think about the details of how you'll shoot it, which is the scripting stage. Most corporate, promotional, or instructional videos are thoroughly scripted and vetted by a good number of people before production even begins. Be careful about deviating during shooting from this type of tightly scripted video. Too many committees of stakeholders will descend on you, and you'll find yourself explaining your choices again and again, and making changes again and again.

Recce

Recce (pronounced RE-kee) is a contraction of *reconnaissance* and is important for any smaller production. Even on a news story, the recce is an essential component of the pre-production process.

What is a recce, and what should you do on one? Ideally you have a checklist of ideas to look for which should go something like this:

1 Name of the production or shoot

2 Name and address of the location

3 Name of the contact person: who gave permission to use the location and who has the keys to access the location

4 Directions: how to get to the location and where to park

5 At the location, check for the time of day you will be shooting: note the angle of the sun or available daylight, how it will shine on your subjects, or which windows it will be coming through

6 Check for power: location, number, and capacity of electrical outlets

7 Check for lighting needs: how much and what type of additional lighting will be needed

8 Check for audio needs: what the acoustics are like, what microphones or sound equipment will be needed

When you have completed your recce, prepare a sheet that details all the information you have gathered and make sure everyone involved with the production gets a copy.

Documentary

There are many different types of productions. In the chapter on editing we looked a little at working on and putting together video with music. In later chapters we'll look at other forms, but in this chapter we'll concentrate on the documentary form.

Obviously different types of productions overlap to some extent or other, and all go through part or all of the pre-production process. Documentary is a loosely used term for factual film or video production. Generally these are productions that present facts and have a narration, either a disembodied voice or one made up from those appearing in the video. Documentaries are the type of shows you might see on the Discovery Channel or National Geographic. Documentary, news, reportage, informational, and even instructional videos are all variations of the same type of video.

Documentaries fall into two main groups: programs that are tightly scripted to start, shot to a prewritten narration, and edited from that, with few changes along the way; or programs that are wholly made up in the editing room, with a structure and a narration that is crafted to fit the material. Many documentaries fall somewhere in between. Even wedding videos are forms of documentary production. In the purest sense they document an event but often include other material that records the couple's background. Wedding videos come in a great many styles and use a great variety of techniques. The ceremony is the tightly scripted portion of the production, while the reception might be largely unscripted.

As rehearsals are to drama productions, so research is to documentary or any other production on location. Documentaries obviously are based on research. You need to know as much as you can about your subject before you even begin writing the script. Because documentary scripts may not get much beyond a treatment, thorough research needs to be done even before the concept is put forward. Research needs to be done not only on the topic itself but also on the production requirements. What's it going to take to spend six months living with the Inuits? What will be needed in terms of cold-weather equipment and clothing? How will you get there, and more importantly how will you get back? How will you keep your camera from turning into a block of ice? How will you protect your precious film or tapes during shooting? This is all part of research beyond the obvious part of what Inuit life is like these days. How much difference is there from group to group? Do you want to emphasize one group over another, play down the differences, or concentrate on the differences? There are an almost infinite number of questions, from the very broad to the very detailed.

In its unscripted form the documentary is very much created by the producer, director, and camera operator on location and then by the editor in the cutting room. Good, experienced camera operators, whether they realize it or not, are actually scripting the story as they shoot it. Certainly every good news camera operator is shooting with the narrator's voice reading the lines in his head. Chances are if it isn't shot for any particular purpose, it will probably not find any use at all. Once the materials have been shot it's the director's and editor's responsibility to bring from that material all that it has to offer.

Documentary can be a factual, accurate representation of events, or it can be an imaginative, poetical, loose interpretation of reality. Either way, documentary can start fully scripted, wholly unscripted, or something in between. One feature that both forms have in common is the tendency to shoot much more material than necessary, sometimes with shooting ratios as high as 25:1, even 100:1, for instance 25 hours or more of shot material for one hour of a finished production.

Editing the Documentary

Many documentary scripts aren't written so much as found, or so says my friend Loren Miller, and there's much truth to that. The mass of material in a documentary is often best sorted out on paper before actual editing. The paper edit is crucial, and the paper edit is the mining for the script that's in the material, Michelangelo finding the statue that's in the stone. The paper edit can be done from transcripts, from log notes, on an Excel spreadsheet, or on 3×5 cards. The idea is always the same: move the information around, find the links, find what flows together, find the conflicts, the drama, and visual strength in the material and put it together into a coherent plan that can be taken into the cutting room.

In loosely scripted documentary material, after working through various shot orders, the frames themselves seem to impose a continuity by being adjacent to each other. Certain shots will seem to want to go together. Then groups of images coalesce into clusters, and the clusters form logical strings, until the whole is built out of the parts and a structure has imposed itself on the material.

Organizing your material is crucial to working efficiently in the documentary form. Well-organized bins with many notes throughout are more than beneficial; they're mandatory. The unscripted documentary benefits greatly from the advent of nonlinear editing systems. Not only do these edit systems give the editor powerful search tools, but they also allow quickly trying many combinations of images. You can try different sequences and archive them, trying different structures and combinations of scenes and scene orders. Though this is an extremely useful tool, try to avoid taking this to extremes. Avoid keeping 20 different versions of your program, as it's easy to get into a muddle and lose track of what's in what sequence. Don't start a new version of a sequence every few edits. You'll probably find yourself getting confused or at least undecided about which to use. It's better to keep substantially different versions of a sequence or a show. As a documentary develops, an idea for a structure of the material may come up, seem like a good idea at the time, but then lead to a muddle later on, forcing you to backtrack to an earlier version which flowed better and worked better as a whole. Because the structure of a documentary can change many times and radically before it's completed, probably much more so than for most narrative films, keep these major changes as separate sequences. For simplicity's sake, on a large project it's better to archive them as entirely separate project files.

Organizing the Clips

Whether it's documentary work, feature production, or a school video yearbook, any production over 15 minutes in length is going to require some organization of your material. If you can organize your material into a coherent pattern of folders and clips you'll go a long way toward making the post-production flow smoothly. There are no firm rules about this, and each project tends to dictate its own organizational structure. The first thing you'll want to do is to capture your material, bring it into your computer, and cut it up into shots. Once you've got it cut up, you should spend some time getting it put away so that you can find it again. You begin with one folder or bin that holds all the master shots. These are usually pretty big chunks of video: 10, 20, 30 minutes. This master bin holds all the reels of material. Avoid capturing whole reels. If there are problems with the digital media, all of it will have to be recaptured. Generally capturing in 15- to 20-minute blocks works well, depending on how it was shot and where there's a natural break. This material gets stored in the master bin as clip *001a*, *001b*, *002a*, *002b*, *002c*, *003a* and so on, the number being the reel number and the letter suffix a piece of that reel.

From the master shots, clips are separated into bins. Keeping the master shots has the advantage that you can go back to the material in bulk to look through it again. As the project nears completion, it's a good idea to go over your material again to see if you overlooked or discarded anything, which can be useful in light of the way the material gets cut together.

The separate bins can be organized in a variety of ways. Tightly scripted projects like narrative film projects that have numbered scenes tend to have material

Figure 7.1 Narrative film organization

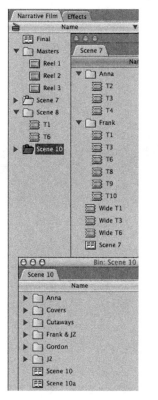

Figure 7.2 Documentary organization

broken down in scene bins, with sub-bins for different types of shots or characters, depending on how complex the scene. So for a narrative project you may have a number of scene bins in addition to your master bin as in Figure 7.1.

The figure shows the beginning development of one method of scene organization. There is a *Masters* bin that holds the three master reels captured so far. Three scenes have been shot, and there are three corresponding bins *Scene 7*, *Scene 8* and *Scene 10*. The *Scene 7* bin is open and has been subdivided into two bins *Frank* and *Anna*. In each of those bins would be single shots, probably close-ups, of Frank and Anna with their take numbers. Also in the *Scene 7* bin are three takes of the wide shot and a sequence called *Scene 7*, in which the scene is actually edited together from the wide, cover shots and the close-ups.

You'll also see a bin for *Scene 8*, a short scene, probably a bridging scene, with just two takes. It has no sequence of its own.

Scene 10, the open bin at the bottom of the figure, is a more complex scene with a number of bins for characters, covers, cutaways, and for a sub-scene between two characters. There are also two sequences called *Scene 10* and *Scene 10a*, which are the main scene together with a sub-scene between two characters that may be edited separately and embedded within the sequence *Scene 10*.

These edited sequences *Scene 7* and *Scene 10* together with the bridging shot for *Scene 8* and eventually *Scene 9* when it's shot and captured will all be placed in the sequence called *Final*, which you see at the top of the figure.

Documentary projects tend to break the material down into subject matter: a bin for the tree shots, another for river scenes, another for snow scenes, another for all the interviews, another for narration tracks, another for music, another for graphics as in Figure 7.2, which shows part of a documentary organization. There are no hard and fast rules on how material is organized; the organization is usually determined by the subject matter.

The real trick in organizing your material is to break it down into enough bins so that the material in your project has a logical structure, but not so many bins that it becomes difficult to find material. As you move clips into bins, add notes—lots of them. The more information you include on the clips, the easier it will be to find them. Without organization you can edit a simple 10-minute video, or you can assemble long pieces of a home movies to make a video, but if you want to make a video of a greater length or greater complexity, such as a DVD yearbook, you have to be organized.

Narration

Documentaries generally use a narration track to carry the information, whether it's a disembodied voice of God speaking truths, an ever-present narrator who wanders through the scene, or pieces of interviews. The narration becomes the bed for the video. When writing your narration, relate your words to the pictures. You have to talk about what you're seeing, but not so closely that the narrator is describing what's being seen. The words have to be just different enough not to seem to be a repetition of the pictures but close enough so the audience can directly and effort-

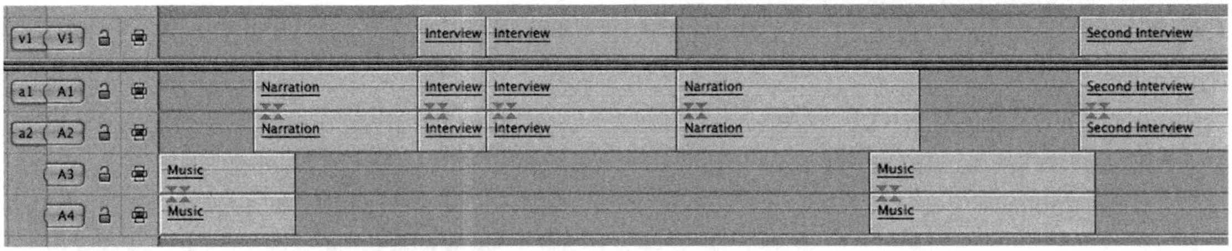

Figure 7.3 Documentary sound bed

lessly relate the two. The narration has to be written slightly off the pictures, but only slightly. Because of this it's critical that the producer and editor find the visual elements that suit and exemplify the words of the narration.

When writing for video, write in an easily understandable, accessible, and conversational style. These are words that are meant to be spoken and heard, not words that are meant to be read. Convoluted sentences, with complex structures, containing sub-clauses and modifying phrases such as this one, while relatively easy to read, are difficult to follow when heard, especially by a disembodied voice.

What many editors like to do is build a bed of the primary audio track and its synchronous video. So if the video starts with a short piece of music, lay down the music on a lower audio track, leaving the primary tracks open for the video. Then the narration comes in. Lay down the narration on a separate track. Then a piece of an interview comes in, so lay in the sound bites in their entirety with the sync picture, jump cuts and all. The picture can always be covered later. Then perhaps more narration, and then another musical break. You can go on and on building the entire soundtrack like this if you wish so it looks something like Figure 7.3. A voice-over feature that allows you to record your narration directly into your computer while watching your video is useful. This is especially handy for recording the kind of scratch track, or rough test narration, to lay down as the basis for the bed.

At this stage, the laid-out video might have a distinctly blocky look to it, but as the material is worked, more and more overlapping of sound and picture will begin to appear.

Some people like to work in a linear fashion, tightly editing the material as they go. It's quite natural to build a sequence this way because this is the natural way a story progresses. On the other hand, I think the benefit of laying out

Recording While You Watch

Another handy use for the ability to record your voice while you're watching your video is simply to make notes. Use headphones to hear your track. Clip on a lavaliere mic as close to your mouth as you can get it, and set off to play your sequence. This is kind of like recording dictation except that it records right into your sequence in line with what you're commenting on. Your comment, "That shot's too dark" appears right underneath the shot that's too dark.

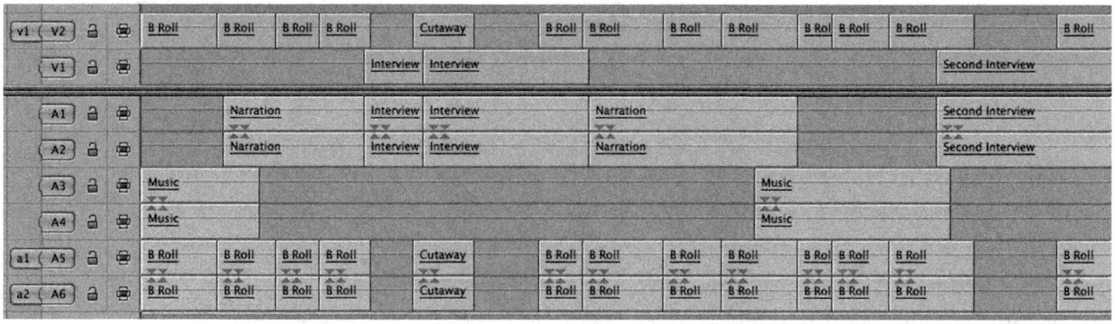

Figure 7.4 B-roll added

the bed is that you get to see what the whole structure is like, where emphasis needs to be placed, where more graphical explanation is needed, where there are parts that may need to be cut because they're taking too much time, or a minor point is being dwelt on too long. Without the whole, it's hard to get that sense of how the material is paced and stands up as a structure.

Once the bed is laid out, the soundtrack flowing smoothly, the content making sense, progressing sensibly from point to point to conclusion like a well-crafted essay, then the pictures are put in to fill the gaps in the track. Having laid down your bed, you're ready to put in the B-roll material. The pacing of the editing is now dictated by language, the rhythm and cadence of speech, which can vary greatly from speaker to speaker, from language to language. Usually it's best to add the B-roll material to track above interview portions if needed. This makes it easier to go back to the interview at a later stage without having to edit it back into the Timeline, which may, in its early stages while the first B-roll material is being added, look something like Figure 7.4.

The bed of course is just a starting block and is not enviable by any means. It's often ripped open to insert natural sound breaks. These are important to let the audience catch its breath and are especially useful when going from one major block in the project to another or from one topic to another.

In practice, an hour-long documentary is usually not laid out as a single bed but rather broken into sequences that are edited separately and then brought together into a final sequence. Opening sequences are often built separately, quite often by entirely separate teams that specialize in motion graphics, 3D, and compositing using tools such as Motion or After Effects.

Editing documentaries is not often about continuity of action but rather about continuity of ideas, putting together images that separately have one meaning but together have a different meaning and present a new idea. This is the concept of montage. The term has come to be used in a few different ways, but the original form established by Russian filmmakers in the 1920s was based on this idea. In this powerful concept you can put together two shots that have no direct relationship with each other and thereby create in the audience's mind a quite different idea, separate from the meaning of its parts. The work of filmmakers like Michael Moore is typical of this type of cutting. This juxtaposition of unrelated images to make the audience draw a continuity of ideas is often done with a sequence of quick, im-

What Is B-roll?

In the old days that were not so long ago, a television anchor or reporter would lay down a commentary track or do an entire on-camera narration, originally as film and later as videotape. Called the A-roll, it would be loaded on a machine, either telecine, which played back film and turned it into video, or VTR. Then shots illustrating the narration would be cut together and loaded on a second machine. This would be the B-roll. Both would be fed into a control room and gang-synced together so that the director could either cut back and forth or use effects to switch between the two. B-roll became the generic term for any cover video, regardless of how it was assembled into the production. B-roll is material that shows what someone is talking about, the shots of the car accident as the police officer describes it, or they can be contrapuntal shots, pictures of wealthy homes while the narration describes poverty in the country. All of these shots serve to illustrate or refine or comment on the narration, interview or other voice over.

B-roll can also be cutaways. Any editor will tell you that cutaways are the most useful shots. You can never have too many, and you never seem to have enough. No editor will ever complain that you have shot too many cutaways. A cutaway shot shows a subsidiary action or reaction that you can use to bridge an edit. It's usually used to contract time. It's the shot of the onlookers watching. It's that overly used shot of a person's hands. The shot of the interviewer nodding in response to an answer is called in England a *noddie*. The noddie allows you to bridge a portion of the interviewee's answer where the person has stumbled over the words or has digressed into something pointless. A wide shot that shows the whole scene can often be used as a cutaway.

pressionistic shots, often with motion. Montage can mean a collection of shots that serve to contract or expand time simply by being cut together. It can be used to create the sense of location or process—for instance, shots of various aspects of car production build up to create an impression of the process. A variety of shots of a town festival produce an effect that gives the flavor of the town and the event. The common trick to make montage effective is fast pacing, using speed to quickly build block on block, shot on shot, to construct the whole. Because of time limitations, montage is often used in commercials. It's a quick and concise way to convey a variety of impressions that make up a single whole.

The juxtaposition of shots with different audio may preclude the use of natural sound because of the harshness of the edit. It often becomes necessary to use unnatural sound or music or to use a split edit to reinforce the point of the intellectual edit. By splitting the sound, the edit happens twice, multiplying its effect. When intercutting material to create tension, what's commonly done is not to cut the sound with the picture, but to keep a constant sound or music to which the editing and the action paces itself.

Music and Narration

A common dilemma that's often posed is whether it is better to cut to the rhythm of the music or to the rhythm of the narration in a sequence. You shouldn't have to be making a choice between the two. If you're having to make that choice, then there is probably something more fundamentally wrong with the sequence. There should either be music, which you're cutting to, or there should be narration. It seldom works to simply slather music under everything, though you see this often, especially in travelogue movies. You should bring the music up for a purpose, and while it's up full, you should be cutting to the music. Then when you bring in the narration, you should fade out the music under the narration. But just keeping it there as a bed to the narration is almost always wrong, unless it's integral to the scene that's being narrated.

If you're having to chose between cutting to one or the other, the music or the narration, then either the music doesn't belong there or it's the wrong narration. Even in a sequence where music is a key element—a video about dance, for instance—you are cutting to the rhythm of the music while the music is up and then to the narration when it's up, even if the music continues underneath. Often with this kind of production, it's better to make the narration quite sparse and punctuated more frequently than you normally would with sections of music. So you get a phrase or a sentence or two at most, then go back to the music and dance briefly, before returning to another short piece of narration. What should be avoided in almost every instance is the tendency to have a blanket of narration lying on top of a blanket of music.

Project: Documentary   This is a major project to create a short documentary about a subject that interests you and is important to your campus community or teen students in general. Though a great deal of latitude can be given in the subject matter, the project may not under any circumstances contain any material that is libelous, defamatory, indecent, harmful, harassing, intimidating, threatening, hateful, objectionable, discriminatory, abusive, or vulgar. No subjects that involve sexual behavior, illegal substance abuse, or offensive racial, cultural, or ethnic content should even be considered.

The video should be approximately three to five minutes in length. It may use shot video, still images, copyright-free music, narration, and titles as are useful for telling the story you want to convey.

1 Working in small groups of four to six you should brainstorm the possibilities and come up with a concept.

2   As in the earlier project, the team will have to present a concept, which has to be approved by the instructor.

3   The next steps are to research the subject in detail and prepare the script. This script will most likely be in treatment, written much like an essay, but including descriptions of the video that will be used and the interviews you might want to include.

4   Once the treatment as been approved, the project can be shot and the necessarily visual elements assembled.

5   The final stage is the recording of the narration and the assembling of the video and audio elements in your editing software.

This project will probably be a significant portion of your class assessment and should be the highest quality and the best work you can produce. It gives you a great deal of freedom, but also requires a great deal of thought, discipline, and care. Excellence should be your goal.

Once the projects have been viewed by your classmates, those the class agrees are worthy shall be viewed by the larger campus community of students, teachers, and administration. Hopefully the productions will also be seen outside the school via broadcast, cable access channels, or other distribution channels.

Lighting

*T*here are three reasons why you light a scene. The first is to provide enough illumination so that your camera can produce a picture. You want to do this without electronically boosting or brightening the image. Though most cameras can electronically boost the video signal, the results are usually grainy and muddy. Sometimes you can use this to create a specific look, but usually you don't want to.

The second reason for lighting is to compensate for your camera's limitations. While the human eye has the ability to see a great range of contrast, the camera does not. It can really see no more than dark gray to pale gray. Fine gradations of darkness or brightness are just not possible with most video cameras without a little help. That's where lighting comes in—to fill those areas of darkness or compensate for the areas of brightness to bring the image into the tolerances the camera allows so the audience sees some detail in both the darker areas of the image as well as in the brighter areas.

The third reason for lighting is to set the tone for the production. If you want your video to be sinister and fearful then you'll probably light it with lots of dark areas and high contrast with patches of light. If you want your video to be more friendly and cheerful you'll light it more brightly, with somewhat more even illumination and brighter colors. Avoid flat, even lighting. This is usually used only for newsrooms and anchor presentations, but even then it is usually too flat and should be avoided. A lot can be done with lighting to set the mood for your production. If an interview is shot in a dark setting, with harsh, dim lighting, the subject will appear sinister and ominous, even threatening. If the same subject is shot in a brightly lit room, with soft, flattering, warm light, he or she will appear friendly, gentle, even loving and romantic. Contrasting colors, splashes of blue light with contrasting warm, orange tones can make a scene look menacing.

Three-Point Lighting

To some degree all film and video lighting is based on what's called three-point lighting. This uses three light sources to illuminate the subject. The three lights are:

1 Key light
2 Fill light
3 Backlight

The main light source is the key light. Outdoors this is usually the sun or the sky. Because we're used to light coming primarily from overhead, even indoors lighting fixtures are usually overhead. The key light is usually set higher than the subject and usually to one side of the camera at about a 45-degree angle or less. You can see this in Figure 8.1. The key light is the primary illumination and is stronger and brighter than the other two. With the key light set like this and the subject facing the camera, one side of the face will be more strongly lit while the other side will be in deep shadow (Figure 8.2). When the light is higher than the subject's head, it might create deep shadows in the eye sockets under the eyebrow, especially

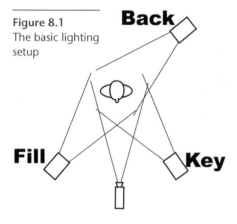

Figure 8.1
The basic lighting setup

Figure 8.2 Key light only

if the eyes are deeply set. Avoid setting the key light too high, creating the Hannibal Lector, *Silence of the Lambs* look. On a subject with prominent cheekbones, there will also be areas of deep shadow under them, as well as under the chin. If you move the key light below the eyeline, the lighting looks quite different. The cheekbone shadow changes, and a small shadow appears between the chin and the mouth. This kind of light is quite unnatural looking and is usually reserved for special effects and for horror movies. If the key light is too angled, too far from the camera line, it will put a large shadow across the subject's shoulder. Bringing the key closer to the camera will reduce the shadow area, having it fall behind the subject rather than on the shoulder.

Anytime you have a single, bright light source, such as one light in a studio, the lighting will be harsh, with sharp, high-contrast shadow areas. This is a type of lighting called low key lighting and is usually used for dramas or gangster movies. It gives the lighting effect that characterizes the *film noir* genre. Low key lighting uses a strong key light with little fill light.

High key lighting is much brighter and more evenly lit, balancing the key light with fill light (Figure 8.3). This is the normal way of shooting and what you'll see every day on television. How much the fill light balances the key light sets the tone for the scene. Little fill light will produce higher contrast, while equal amounts of fill and key will make the scene look evenly lit and flat looking with no contrast. Avoid this type of flat lighting. Your audience is looking at a flat, two-dimensional image. To get some sense of depth and three-dimensionality in the

Figure 8.3 Key light with fill

image it's important to use lighting that creates modeling, giving the subject shape and depth by showing areas of light and shadow. The shadow areas, contrasting with the bright areas, give the image shape and depth. For an average scene the ratio of fill light to key light is usually from 2:1 down to 1.5:1. With this setup, with the key light is twice as bright as the fill light or nearly twice are bright, you will get a nice degree of modeling without too harsh a contrast between the light and dark areas in the shot.

There are a couple of ways to adjust the intensity of the fill light. One way is to use a smaller, less powerful lamp. If the key light is 500 watts, then the fill light might be 250 watts. If the two lights are equal distances from the subject, one light will be twice as bright as the other. If you want the fill to be brighter, move it closer to the subject. The brighter the fill is in relation to the key the more it will soften and reduce the shadow modeling produced by the key light.

There is a law of physics called Newton's Inverse Square Law, which governs light, sound, gravity and other forces. In the case of light the law determines the strength of the light in relation to its distance from the object it's falling on. The math involved in this is the subject of a physics class, but for our purposes the law basically says that the amount of illumination is a square of its distance from the subject. This means that if you double the distance of a light from a subject it will not be half as bright, but only a quarter as bright. So to make a light half as bright, you need to move it a quarter of the distance it currently is from what it's illuminating. With a little practice you'll quickly get the feel for how well your lights illuminate a subject.

Figure 8.4 Backlight only

In most lighting setups, in addition to the key light and the fill light, a third lamp is added to the scene to improve the lighting. This is the backlight. The backlight, as its name implies, goes behind the subject and lights the area on the back of the head and shoulders (Figure 8.4). Once you've set up the backlight, switch it off and on a few times to see the effect it's having on the subject. The purpose of the backlight is to help separate the subject from the background, giving the scene a sense of depth and three-dimensionality. Usually the backlight is set on the same side as the key light, as if the primary illumination was coming from that side. This is especially true of a single-subject setup where the subject is facing the camera. In other setups, the backlight can either be on the fill light side, or as is often the case, suspended directly behind the subject. Care should be taken with the backlight to avoid it shining into the camera lens or producing lens flares on the image. These should be masked off as much as possible with flags attached to the light or the light stand.

Placing and controlling the backlight can be difficult, but it's well worth the effort. How much backlight you use depends most on the subject that's being lit. Subjects with blond or white hair or pale clothing will need will need little backlight, as it will quickly brighten into a halo effect. Subjects with dark hair and dark clothing will need a great deal more backlight to get the effect you want. Try to avoid having pale-haired subjects wear very dark clothing; generally black or bright white clothing is to be avoided in video.

Exercise: Lighting

The lighting exercise is very dependent on available equipment and space. Ideally a number of groups of students should be able to set up three-point lighting situations with the space and lamps available. If not, small groups of two or three should take turns setting, aiming, adjusting, and dismantling the lights for three-point lighting.

1 Set up a classroom monitor so the students can see what the camera sees and the lighting effects that are being produced.

2 Each group should set up a camera on a tripod and connect its output to the monitor.

3 Each team should take turns setting the lights, camera, focus, and exposure for the lighting setup. Each group should do the setup in a different part of the space available so that each team must completely assemble, execute, and disassemble the lighting setup.

4 In addition to being viewed on the classroom monitor, it might be useful to tape the different setups to review later.

The Dark Side

Normally the subject that's being lit does not face directly into the camera; the subject is viewed slightly from one side as if facing someone else, with the camera simply looking on. What often sounds quite counterintuitive to most people is

Figure 8.5 Shooting the dark side

that you normally do not place the key light on the same side of the subject as the camera. The camera is placed on the opposite side and the camera shoots what's called the dark side. You'll see this type of lighting every day in motion pictures and television. Every television interview is shot this way, and almost every scene in movies is shot like this. This lighting setup can be seen in Figure 8.5.

The exposure is usually set to be correct for the center of the face, so the near side tends to be darker, while the side opposite the camera is brighter and might even appear slightly overexposed. If the key and the fill are correctly balanced, the exposure will not be so extreme from the center of the face to the overexposed side, and the dark side will remain in shadow.

Lighting like this gives better separation of the subject from the background because the highlight area is on the far side of the subject. This lighting also requires only a little complimentary backlight. Usually with this type of setup the background is kept darker than the foreground.

This type of lighting setup also has an extra benefit for an interview or a scene between two people. Instead of having three lamps for each subject, only four lamps are used, each key light doubling as a backlight as in Figure 8.6. This type of scene is often shot with two cameras, which makes it easier for the editor to intercut the two shots as necessary.

In the figure there are two cameras, camera 1 on the right is shooting the subject marked X, while camera 2 on the left is shooting the subject marked Y. The two cameras are producing medium shots of the two subjects. X, who is on the left of the scene, is being lit by key light A. The key light on X is being balanced by fill light A. Both lights illuminating X are to the sides of camera 1 and facing the sub-

Figure 8.6 Common interview setup

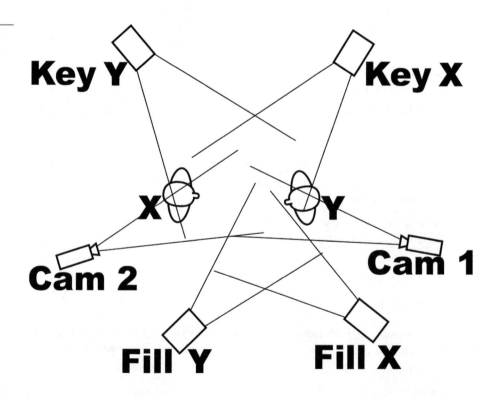

ject. Y is being illuminated by key light B and fill light B; both of these lights are to the sides of the camera facing the subject. The trick to this lighting setup is that key light A, in addition to being the primary light for subject X, also acts as the backlight to subject Y. Similarly, key light B is acting as the backlight for X. Separate backlights can be used, but they're often not necessary if the keys and fills and carefully positioned and balanced. It takes some skill to avoid getting the lights on the opposite side shining into the camera lens, but with a little practice, you should get used to doing it without too much trouble.

Continuity of lighting is important. The crucial elements to control are the key light and the fill. First, make sure the key light is consistently coming from the same side in the scene. If two people are facing each other and the key is falling on the left side of one subject's face, then the key light should fall on the right side of the other subject. This way the light will appear to be coming from the same light source. Second, make sure the key and fill are balanced equally on both subjects. So if one person has a key-to-fill ratio of 2:1, try to have the key-to-fill ratio for the others in the scene be the same. Obviously this is not a hard and fast rule. If someone is supposed to be lurking in the shadows, they'll have less key light on them and perhaps little or no fill. For complex scenes in which the camera is moved around a good deal be especially careful that the light balance and source appear consistent.

Background Lighting

When you're shooting indoors, particularly in a studio, in addition to lighting your subject you will of course have to light the background of the scene as well, unless you want the look of your principal subjects sitting in a pool of blackness. The way you light your background is partly determined by your set and what's in the background. It's a good idea to keep the background uncluttered, with plain walls, simple drapes, or a object or two strategically placed so that it does appear to be in front of someone's nose or coming out of the top of the subject's head. Plain walls and drapes are often enhanced with lighting, creating brighter areas of muted color and areas of darker shadow.

Lighting the background with splashes of light and dark is usually done with one or two lights. These are heavily flagged to shape the light beam to a narrow area. This is done either with barn doors that come with the lamp head and are used to confine the light. The barn doors are often supplemented with black wrap (Figure 8.7). Black wrap can be purchased from camera supply stores and is a sheet of aluminum foil spray-painted matte black, which can be cut into pieces and used as necessary to block off light from areas where you don't want it to fall.

In addition to shaping the light that falls on the background, lighting directors often cover the lamps with colored gels to produce different light streaks on the background. It's quite common for backgrounds to be made in neutral gray for the walls and drapes. These are then washed with colored light to create the effect the lighting director wants.

As well as basic streaks and patches of light, colored or not, specific shapes are often used. Film and video supply stores carry a variety of these cookies in an

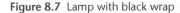

Figure 8.7 Lamp with black wrap

Figure 8.8 Cookie
(Courtesy Mole-Richardson Co.)

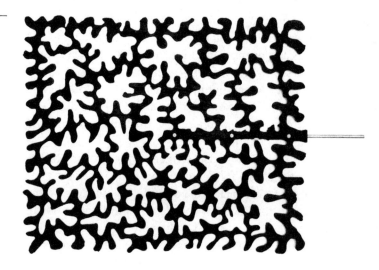

assortment of masks that create shadows like Venetian blinds, palm trees, bare branches, ornate fretwork, and much more (Figure 8.8). You can also use black wrap to create your own.

■ *Note:* The mattes used in film and video to create interesting shadow shapes are called cookies not because they're round and edible but because they're named after a Greek lighting grip in Hollywood called Cucoloris, who first used them. Though still often called Cucoloris, they're more commonly simply called cookies.

It is important for the lighting director and camera operator to understand the importance of lighting continuity to maintain good color and tonal balance across the shots within a scene. Different manufacturers do make their cameras with quite different color and lighting responses. Intercutting shots between cameras that have different color characteristics will be obvious to the audience and needs to be corrected either with careful lighting or in post-production. Even when cameras from the same manufacturer are used it's important that they be color balanced to match each other. It's best to do this by comparing the cameras on the same monitor. Ideally this is done on a monitor with multiple inputs that allow you to switch quickly from one to the other. Do this first using color bars that are shot by each camera, not simply generated within the camera. Compare these to see if the camera reproduction is identical. Then compare the shots of the scene itself to see if they reproduce the scene with the same colors and tone. When working with one camera it's important to make sure that the skin tones of the subjects are color balanced correctly and consistently from shot to shot within the scene. This is especially important because we all know approximately what correct flesh tone color is. The background is less critical because your audience has probably never seen it before, so you can make it any color you want, but flesh has to be flesh-colored or it looks like you're creating a special effect. If you do use lighting for special effects, giving a scene a blur or a yellow cast, be careful to make it consistent across the scene and across those in the scene.

Hard Light and Soft Light

One of the most important aspects of lighting is to control the type of light falling on the subject. Light can be either hard light or soft light. Hard light (Figure 8.9a) is light that produces sharp, distinct, hard-edged shadows. The sun on a bright day produces hard light. Streetlights usually produce hard light. This means there are sharp, harsh contrasts between areas of light and dark. Soft light (Figure 8.9b) produces soft shadows with indistinct edges. An overcast day will give you soft light. Fluorescent lights are usually soft light. Hard light is often used in drama or suspense to emphasize the importance or gravity of a situation. Soft light is much more flattering and used for most productions to minimize wrinkles and blemishes. It's used in light drama or comedy as it gives a more relaxed look to the image. This is not to say that every shot in a drama is shot with hard light and every shot in a comedy with soft light but that those genres usually use those types of lighting.

Generally fill lights are softened more than key lights. If the fill is too hard you'll get multiple, sharp shadows on the subject's features, which can look quite unpleasant. If the fill light is too strong, almost equal to the key, you create a shadow light down the center of the subject's nose. Softening the key will set the type of lighting for the scene, while softening the fill will simply prevent excessive shadowing. Try to avoid using too many lights, as multiple shadows from many light sources can look quite unnatural. Some lighting directors like to work with a lot of small lamps, each illuminating specific areas of the scene. This can

Figure 8.9a Hard light

Figure 8.9b Soft light

Figure 8.10a Photoflex MovieDome

Figure 8.10b Photoflex SilverDome soft box kit

Figure 8.10c Photoflex soft boxes in action

Figure 8.11 Videssence fluorescent bank

look spectacular, but it takes great skill and a good deal of careful, patient work to produce good results that don't look like a mess.

Many lighting kits come with a collection of lamps that are quite strong, difficult to control, and which produce a hard light. This can be unpleasant to work with, requiring careful placement to fill and soften the lights' hard-edged shadows. Many photographers prefer to work with lights that produce a softer light. There are lights available that do this easily. Called soft boxes, they often go by a brand name. Chimera and Photoflex are two of the most common. Figure 8.10a shows the Photoflex MovieDome, which is a large soft box that illuminates a large area evenly. Figure 8.10b is the Photoflex SilverDome kit that uses smaller lights and is excellent for interviews. Figure 8.10c shows the Photoflex soft boxes in action. Soft boxes are designed with lamps inside soft, reflective frames and covered with thin gauzy scrims that diffuse the light. These lights produce soft shadows that are look good, are easy to work with, and flattering on the subject. Most news studios are lit either with these types of lights or specially designed fluorescent lamps such as the Videssence (Figure 8.11) that produce an exceptionally even but naturally colored light.

Figure 8.12 Diffuser

Even if you don't have soft boxes or other special soft lighting, the standard lighting kit can be made to create the soft light look. This is done by using pieces of fine-spun fiberglass, because they're heat-resistant, to cover the light, diffusing and softening it (Figure 8.12). Larger diffusion screens are mounted on separate stands, while smaller ones are clipped to the barn doors of a light, with wooden (not plastic) clothes pegs because they're heat-resistant. Often double or even triple layers of spun fiberglass are needed to diffuse a lamp to the level achieved by soft boxes. This of course means a considerable light loss, so a stronger lamp might be necessary, or one that's closer to the subject might be necessary.

As with key and fill lights, it's important that the type of lighting used, hard or soft, remain consistent within a scene. Avoid having one subject lit with hard light while someone else is softly lit. However flattering this might look, it will also cut together awkwardly.

Filters

Filters are useful especially to help improve shooting scenes outdoors. Try to get an ultraviolet (UV) filter for your lens. Not only does it serve to protect the delicate lens coating from dust and scratches, but it also makes color outdoors a little richer and more vibrant while reducing haze in long shots.

Another useful filter is a polarizing filter. Like the UV filter they help to cut through haze as well as enriching color saturation, but they also have the added benefit of reducing glare and reflections such as those you get off water or other shiny surfaces. They also have the effect of making blue skies more vivid.

Neutral-density filters are often important for working outdoors. ND filters are often built into better cameras. Outdoors, most cameras will produce exposure with a small aperture at high f-stop numbers. As we have seen this is a factor in the amount of depth of field that appears in the shot. Unless the f-stop can be reduced, opening the aperture wider than is normal outdoors, the depth of field will always be from a few inches to the far horizon. There are two ways to do this: use a neutral density filter, or turn up the shutter speed.

The neutral-density filter will reduce the level of the light reaching the lens while having no effect on the color of the image. These filters come in various densities. For a consumer camera a heavy ND filter is needed to reduce the aperture on a bright day.

The shutter speed of most video cameras is normally 1/60th of a second. Increasing the shutter speed, reducing the amount of time the light has to enter the camera, will force the camera to open the iris to allow enough light to enter. Many cameras now have shutter speeds down to 1/10,000th of a second. These are excellent for reducing exposure.

■ *Note:* High shutter speeds are useful for shooting sports events. What the fast shutter does is produce images that are crisp and sharp. If you take a picture at 1/60th of a second of something moving at high speed, during that 1/60th of a second the image will be blurred as it moves. If, however, you take the same picture at 1/10,000th of a second, there is almost no motion in that time, making the image sharp and clean. This is especially useful if you later want to slow down the shot. Any slow motion in post-production will look better if it's based on shots that were taken with a high shutter speed. These fast shutter speeds are of course suitable only outdoors where there's a lot of light and may not work in gyms that are not adequately lit.

It's common for lighting directors to use filters to alter the color of a scene, to give a shot a bluish cast or to warm the look of a shot. However, unless you're certain of what you want, it's better to do color changes to the image in post-production rather than while you're shooting.

Black mist filters are used to soften a scene, making it look a little dreamy and romantic, putting a slight glow around highlight areas. This filter is often used on close-ups to give a more flattering look to the subject. Other special-effects filters include star and fog filters. Star filters use etched patterns to spread highlights into star-shaped points of light, while fog filters produce a heavy softening of the light as if shot through a heavy fog.

Lighting Situations

So far we've looked at lighting setup and lighting in a general way. Let's now look at lighting for different types of situations: the studio, the location, and outdoors.

Studio Lighting

Much of what we've seen so far applies to working in the studio. Many studios, newsroom sets in particular, are lit evenly to the point of the lighting being flat with little or no model of features. This is used because it helps to mask lines, wrinkles, blemishes, and sagging skin. This is why many news studios use fluorescent lighting system, which are even and soft.

Though studio lighting is artificial, it's sometimes beneficial to try to recreate lighting that appears natural, as if the light is coming from a source such as a window or an overhead light or a bedside lamp. Think in terms of how a light source illuminates a scene. If you can't imagine it, see if you can find the same illumination in real life and take a still picture of it. This will help you visualize the type of light the source produces and how light and shadow affect the subject and the background.

Studios ideally are equipped with some kind of lighting grid to which lights can be suspended so they are out of the way and off the floor. Before you mount an elaborate lighting grid make sure your electrical system will support the lighting load you're going to put on it. Count up the wattage of your total number of lights. Divide that by 100, and you'll have the amperage load of all your lamps. This means that a total of 2,000 watts can be supported on a 20-amp circuit.

It will probably be necessary to spread the load to make sure that not all the current is coming from a single circuit. Hopefully the studio will have sufficient outlets and sufficient strength to sustain the loads you'll put on it.

Once you've figured out how you'll distribute the load to the outlets around the studio space it's time to put up the lighting grid. This can be an elaborate system with powered mounts that will raise and lower the lamp heads, or more likely a few rows of pipes, securely mounted to the ceiling beams or support structure. It's important that this be soundly secured and engineered to support the necessary weight. The pipe grid is hung a few feet from the ceiling itself, allowing space for heat to dissipate from the lamp heads.

The pipe rows should be positioned so that they line up where you want your key and fill lights to be and another row that you want to use for your backlights. A couple of additional sections of pipe as well as crossing sections should be mounted to allow different lighting positions for a cross-lit interview as well as providing background lighting.

Each lamp that's mounted on the lighting grid should be securely clamped to the grid and chained to the pipes with a safety chain. The cabling from the lamps should run along the pipes and be tie-wrapped to them. The cables should go to the outer walls, run down the walls, and be secured to the walls.

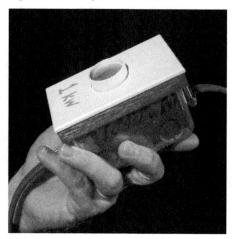

Figure 8.13 Simple in-line dimmer

All the lights should be fed into a theatrical dimmer that will allow control of each lamp's strength and also allow you to fade out the lights. If a full theatrical dimmer is not possible, a heavy-duty in-line dimmer switch on each light cable will give you great control on the overall lighting and allow you to adjust the look of any scene (Figure 8.13). Put each dimmer on the cable near where it's plugged into an outlet. If dimmers are not available, mount the lamps on the grid in the most pleasing arrangement of key, fill and backlight you can manage, and balance the strength of the various lamps.

With the lighting grid and dimmers you should be able to create most of the lighting styles you'll want to achieve, with minimum repositioning of lamps, while keeping the floor free of stands and cables.

Location Lighting

Often, you won't be able to shoot in the studio. You'll be required to shoot in less-than-ideal circumstances and in locations that give you less-than-optimal control of the lighting. Here the principal problem is to generate enough light. The standard lighting kit often produces light that, though bright, is too harsh in a confined space. To soften the light a common technique is to take a bright lamp, and, instead of aiming it directly at the subject, point it at the ceiling, so the light is reflected. This will produce a general, even, soft overall light. This even works for larger areas, using a number of lamps. This is often the simplest way to create enough illumination to get a good image. A white ceiling will make a great reflector, providing near shadow-free lighting. This light should be supplemented with key and backlights to create modeling and background separation. The overall lighting level should give sufficient fill to balance a weak key light, which is really used just to punch a little more light into a specific area of the scene.

Power drain is especially important to check on location. Many homes and offices will be able to support only 15 to 20 amps on a single circuit. If there is already office equipment on the circuit adding another 2,000 watts of lights will probably overload the circuit. It's a good idea to switch off as much office equipment and lighting, and to run long extension cords to other areas that are on other circuits to spread the amperage load as much as possible.

Sometimes no additional lighting will be possible. You'll be forced to use only the available lighting, for example, at basketball games or theatrical performances. Gyms are notorious for being poorly lit or lit with low-cost lighting that produces truly dreadful color reproduction in film and video cameras. In these cases there is nothing that can be done except to color balance as best you can and use the color correction tools of your editing system to fix it best as possible. Often even this isn't enough as these lighting systems produce light that is missing portions of the full light spectrum, making it nearly impossible to recreate them in the final output of your video.

Theatrical lighting usually uses full-spectrum lights but often at low levels with high contrast with the rest of the image. Theatrical lighting directors are usually reluctant to raise levels necessary to create good pictures in the camera. In most cases you'll be able to get by with the lighting provided. Two points to be careful of are the high contrast of the scene and the shallow depth of field you're often forced to work with. Set your exposure carefully and make sure auto iris is not active. The same applies to focus. It's important that auto focus is switched off, as the shallow depth of field will easily create breathing in the focus adjustment. Be careful also of the color balance. Theatrical productions are often lit with gelled lights that produce different color sources on the subject. Avoid using auto white balance so that the color response of the camera doesn't appear to be changing as the lighting changes. It's better to have a fixed color balance and allow the theatrical lighting to affect the scene as intended, even if this might look quite garish in video reproduction. You might be able to tone it down in finishing during post-production.

Outdoor Lighting

Most people think that lighting outdoors is not necessary for video production, that the natural daylight will provide all the illumination you need. Unfortunately, though a powerful light source, the sun is also a harsh source and presents serious challenge to anyone trying to shoot an optimal image for a video camera.

One problem with the sun is that it keeps moving, so shadows move with it. At noon the sun is high and produces deep shadows under the eyebrow ridges. With deeply set eyes these can look like black, empty holes in the face. Shadows form under the cheeks and under the tip of nose. Later in the afternoon the shadows are falling across the face, now producing sharp, pronounced dark areas to left or right of the nose. Intercutting this material with the shots taken at noon can look awkward.

The sun as a key light also produces hard, deep, sharp-edged shadows that are not very attractive or flattering to the subject. It's important to add some fill light. The easiest way to do this is with a reflector (Figure 8.14). There are commercially available reflectors that can be used to fill the shadow areas. These come

Figure 8.14 Reflector used with diffuser

in a variety of shapes and sizes with different types of reflective surfaces, from bright, shiny silver to a softer white reflector, to a soft golden reflector that creates a warmer fill light.

Be careful with large reflectors, especially if there's a breeze blowing, as they become difficult to control. Making the fill light move as it reflects on the subject can create the effect of reflections off water, but usually it's distracting.

Commercial reflectors can be folded into a protective carrying bag, which is convenient, but it's fairly easy to make your own reflectors. One commonly used reflective surface is simple white foam core. It's light, almost too light to handle in a wind, but it makes a nice, even, soft reflection that for closer shots works well as a fill light. A strong reflector can be created by using aluminum foil. Often attached to one side of the foam core, it gives a stronger reflection than the white surface. Putting it on the back of the foam core gives you two options for different reflective surfaces on one board.

To use the reflector place it as close to the subject as you can get without interfering with the shot, on the side away from the sun, angled upward to catch the bright light and bounce it back into the subject's eye sockets. As you position it, move it around to see how it's falling on the subject to get the optimal amount of reflection just where you want it to fall. Once you've found the sweet spot, it's important to hold the reflector as steady as possible to keep the light from moving around.

Reflectors work best for medium shots and close-ups, where they're most important. For long shots they'll have little effect, as the reflection spreads too quickly from the point source on the surface of the reflector.

Though reflectors are good for improving exterior lighting, they can be strong and difficult for actors to work with. The bright light shining directly into the face and eyes makes it hard for them to avoid squinting, but with a little practice it can be done for short periods.

Another technique for working outdoors is to avoid shooting in direct sunlight but to shoot in shaded areas. This is easier on the subjects, as it's cooler and they don't have the bright light of the sun or of bright reflectors to contend with. Shaded areas provide a softer, more constant light. The problem here is that you might have to contend with bright sunlit areas in the background. These will tend to be overexposed. With careful shot placement, you should be able to minimize or avoid their impact on the composition.

What also works well, for shorter scenes or where only a few shots are needed, is to shoot in the early hours of the morning or late in the afternoon. Both of these can produce pleasing color casts to the image, with a softer light. Avoid shooting under direct sunlight between 10 a.m. and 3 p.m. or even later in the summer. During this time the sun is too high to produce a pleasant image without a lot of extra fill light.

Another solution that works well, either when shooting in the sunlight or when shooting in shade is to use a lighting kit to enhance and complement the daylight. In the sun, the lights will serve as fill to compensate and soften the bright light. In the shade, the lights often act as the key, adding an extra punch or highlight to the shot, brightening up the subject more strongly than the shadow areas that provide the overall lighting. The latter technique can produce excellent results, but both require that you be close enough to a power source. One other point to be aware of when dealing with using lights outdoors is that they are usually rated with the color temperature of tungsten lights. This is a much warmer, more yellow light than daylight. When mixing artificial light with daylight it's usually necessary to gel the tungsten lights with a blue filter to balance the color temperature of normal daylight.

There is one other technique that works well but requires great care. Camera manuals tell you to shoot with the sun behind the camera so that it lights the subject. This illuminates the scene but produces deep, harsh shadows in direct sunlight as we've seen. By turning the scene around, shooting with the sun coming from behind the subject, the hard shadows are avoided. The subject's face is much more softly lit by the reflected daylight, while the brightness of the sun acts as a strong backlight. Exposure must be set for the face and not for the overall scene, or the subject is liable to turn into a silhouette. This illuminates the hair and shoulders, creating excellent three-dimensionality and separation from the background, which tends to be overly bright. A reflector can be added to push a little more light into the face. It's an attractive, flattering way of staging a scene, but you have to be careful about getting the sun or flares from the lens on the image. It can be tricky to balance foreground to background, shadow to light, but if used properly it can produce outstanding images.

Composition

Composition is an important element for a lighting director or camera operator to consider when setting the lighting for a shot or a scene. In every composition there should be balance, areas of light and areas of darkness. In most shots you want to avoid creating an image that's uniform, whether light, dark, or neutral. A dark object in the shot should be balanced with a light object or a light area. Similarly it is a good idea to balance the weight of objects. That's not the physical weight but the apparent weight. A large object in the frame seems heavier than a smaller object and may need to be balanced, or the shot might seem lopsided. As you balance areas of light and dark you should be aware that the audience's eyes will initially be drawn to the areas of brightness. This is why in most compositions you'll see the primary subject be more lit, perhaps even be in a pool of light, while surrounded objects will be slightly darker. Sometimes, especially in interviews, this is obvious, but even in other scenes you'll see this technique used to some extent or other.

Different shapes and lines within the frame have different strengths and weaknesses. It's important to understand that not every composition has to be a forceful, strong composition. It's often useful to alternate compositional elements, especially when they can be used to emphasize character and story. Within a composition, horizontal lines and shallow, slow curves are gentle, restful, or weak. Traditional landscapes, with their long, straight, horizontal lines, are calming and restful. On the other hand, compositions with diagonal lines in the frame, or

Figure 8.15 Dingleberry shot

triangular compositions, are forceful and stronger. Portraits are often painted with strong diagonal shapes in the frame; areas of light and dark bisect areas of the frame in diagonal lines. While low camera angles, looking up at subjects, emphasize strength and power, high angles convey submissiveness or weakness. Lighter, brighter tones, and the use of high key lighting are generally weaker, more open, and calming. Darker tones and the use of low key lighting are commanding, conveying strength, forcefulness, and dignity.

It's common for camera operators when shooting a landscape scene to frame the composition, often using a dark branch at the top of the image, together perhaps with a tree on one side to frame a shot. The overhanging branch serves not only as a frame to the image but also helps to reduce the amount of bright sky in the shot, helping with exposure control if the sky is very bright and nicely drawing the audience to the main element in the composition. This hanging branch is often referred to as a dingleberry (Figure 8.15). If you don't have a tree available for this purpose, you can always bring your own branch and have someone out of shot hold it so that's it's just dangling into the top of the frame.

Be careful with this technique and don't overdo it, as dark areas at the top of frame can appear oppressive, bearing down on the frame, giving the image a sinister look. You'll often see this technique used when shooting landscapes in drama. Normally these shots are restive and calming, but to maintain the tension a graduated filter that darkens the sky is used to give the image a more sinister look, maintaining the tension. Using lighter, brighter tones at the top of frame makes the image look more airy and open, even cheerful when compared to the darkness at the top of the image. Though this comes from our view of sky and how we relate to it, it nonetheless applies to every shot. If the upper part of a room is in shadow the scene will appear sinister. This is commonly seen in gangster movies and when using low key lighting. If the light brightens toward the top of the frame, the scene will seem more relaxed and less threatening. Commonly in romantic comedies you don't see shadow areas in the upper part of rooms. Rather they are evenly lit with high key lighting that produces no shadow areas on the walls and especially not near the top edges of the frame. Intimate scenes however will use a low key technique but are usually careful to balance the light and dark in the frame to avoid the scene appearing sinister.

The director and the camera operator should be aware of lines in the shot, such as a road, power lines, or the rows of windows in a building. These lines, whether straight or curved, will draw the viewer's eyes in a specific direction. They should be used to draw the audience toward what's important in the shot. If the lines in the image simply traverse the composition, the viewer's eyes will tend to follow them and end up being led nowhere. The lines then serve no purpose but act as a distraction. If the lines cannot be used to benefit the composition, try to reframe the shot or stage the scene in such a way that they can be excluded.

Color is another important factor to be aware of in your shots. Someone wearing a bright red dress will draw the audience's eyes, especially if it's surrounded by dull colors or areas of darkness. If you don't want the audience to focus on the dress in the background, it would be better to either re-costume the person or to reframe the composition. When you are thinking about costuming, don't just think about what your lead actors will wear, but think also about what will be worn by those in the background. Color obviously doesn't only come from costumes. You need to be aware when you're composing a shot or lighting a scene how objects in the scene might dominate the composition. If there is something colorful in the background, you might want to put less light on that area to tone it down so it has less impact on the shot.

Action

9

An important technique to learn is how to shoot action. By this I don't only mean movies like a *Terminator* or a *Lord of the Rings*. There is action in every form of production, every feature, short narrative, and even in some documentaries and other types of video. All forms of video use elements and techniques of action, where what occurs in one shot continues smoothly into the next, when you are staging a scene and cutting for continuity of action. While documentary is often based on non-continuous shots and juxtaposes apparently unrelated images, action films are based, within each scene, almost exclusively on continuity, a smoothness that makes the film appear seamless. The director has to shoot the scene so that the elements match as precisely as possible, that movements repeat as exactly as possible, that the appearance of people and things (and the content of objects like beer glasses) change as little as possible from shot to shot. Shooting action is working to find a smooth way to transition from one part of the action to the next. While editing, action is often about finding that precise moment that matches two events together as closely as possible.

What's critical to shooting and editing action is to create a continuous flow of direction and staging. This is where the Rule of the Line that we saw in Chapter 5 becomes of crucial importance. The director must keep the camera on one side of the line. You can move the camera anywhere you want within the 180-degree angle of arc that defines one side of the line. As long as you follow this rule, you are going a long way toward being able to produce smooth continuity of action.

The basis of directing and editing this type of production is to allow the change from one shot to the next to take place during a movement. Pretty much any action can be used to disguise this type of edit:

- The moment when someone walks in the door
- When someone sits in the chair
- When the hero pulls the heroine into his arms

A turning head or a laugh can be effective cutting points. Something as simple as rising from a table is almost always used to disguise an edit and change the emphasis of a scene. The director's blocking of the actors, the staging of who moves where, sits where, when they rise and do some business, all of this is used to move the audience through the drama or action of the scene, and the editor uses these significant actions that have been blocked out as useful cutting points to move the audience from character to character and action to action.

It's one of these types of moments that the director and the editor use to draw the audience into the scene or back them out of it. When you're cutting on action there are three possible places to cut the movement. You can cut:

- Just before the action takes place
- During the action itself
- After the action is completed

Each of the shot changes has a different meaning for the audience and acts in a different way. Whenever you cut on action it is important that not only the size of the shot change but also that the angle of the shot change, at least 30 to 40 degrees from the previous shot.

- If you cut to a closer shot from a wider shot and put the shot change before the action begins, this emphasizes the action or movement itself.
- If you make the same cut from a closer to a wider shot after the action is completed; this emphasizes not the action but the object or person you're cutting to. Cutting before the action begins or after the action is completed makes the edit more pointed, more apparent to the audience.
- If you make the cut during the movement, the edit tends to be hidden by the movement. This shot change is probably the preferred edit in many circumstances.

Sometimes it is important to mark the event before it occurs. Sometimes it is necessary not to disrupt the action but to let it complete before we move on. Sometimes it's best to make the action flow as smoothly as possible, to conceal the edit within the movement. As a rule of thumb, cutting on action works best when the cut comes about two-thirds of the way through the movement rather than right after the movement starts or at the midpoint. That way the movement just finishes in the second shot. Cutting before an action generally works better when moving from a closer to a wider shot, rather than vice versa. None of these rules are by any means hard and fast. Every situation will vary; every cut will be different and require a different decision. These are the decisions you have to make as a director when you're staging a scene and as an editor when the scene is being cut.

A mistimed edit can be frustrating for the audience, but if done carefully it can be used to build tension. Take this scene:

A man is seated behind a desk. We hear a knock on the door. The man looks up. We cut to the door, which opens as a woman enters saying, "May I come in?" By placing the cut in the natural moment when the man looks up there is no tension built in the scene.

In the same scene, the man is behind the desk. There is a knock on the door. The man looks up, and we hear a woman say, "May I come in?" Then we cut to the woman standing at the door. The delay in the edit builds a subtle anticipation and tension in the audience.

■ *Note:* The only exception to the cutting on movement rule, which is a hard and fast rule, is to not cut during lip movement. The mouth should be closed and the word complete on the frame on which the cut takes place. Cutting during lip flap can be quite disconcerting, like you're cutting someone off in mid-speech. Even if you're not cutting the sound, cutting while the mouth is starting to open can be annoying. This is most noticeable in close-ups, but it's something you should be aware of even in medium or long shots.

The Chase

A great way to practice planning, shooting, directing, and cutting action is to stage a chase scene. The chase offers a variety of technical and production problems that are important to learn to deal with. You have to prepare to maintain continuity in lighting, props, costuming, and most importantly, in direction. If you want to maintain for the audience the illusion that A is chasing after B, the direction of movement has to be as constant as possible, and any changes in direction have to be shown to the audience and explained. Together with continuity of direction goes continuity of action. If someone goes around a corner in one shot, we can't wait for the person to come around the corner in the next. There would be a loss of continuity, like a lapse of time that would look unnatural. Every effort in staging, directing, and cutting this type of scene goes into making the events and the timing seem natural. So when the chaser goes around the corner in one shot, he or she is picked up coming around the corner in the next shot. Timing is essential to maintain continuity of action. You can't have your pursuer closing in on the prey in one shot and suddenly seem to have fallen behind in the next. A bit of directorial business needs to be staged to explain this, such as a brief stumble by the pursuer or a momentary hesitation in which way to go.

Inherent in most every chase scene is the concept of parallel action, intercutting two events or locations that the audience sees as happening simultaneously.

For instance, when we see the pursuer and then a shot of the person being pursued, we assume that the two actions are happening at the same time. What characterizes most chase sequences is that they reach the climax where there is a convergence of time and place, where the pursuer reaches the pursued. Even if the pursued person escapes, to fulfill the build up of the scene it's important that the two antagonists meet in time and place in one location. Think of the parallel action drawing the two closer and closer together till they meet.

For the editor of this type of action scene, in addition to tightly maintaining action continuity, he or she will want to enhance the scene by having it build toward a climax, when either the prey is caught or escapes. This can be done with a variety of techniques, the most common being to accelerate the cutting, so the scene, which might start out relatively slowly, gets cut faster and faster, with shorter and shorter shots, driving the audience toward the climax. As the cutting accelerates it becomes more and more important that each shot carry a significant piece of information with the minimum amount of screen time. Make the shot last as long as it needs to be to tell the audience what you want and not a frame longer. As soon as the visual information is conveyed, you can cut out of the shot.

One technique that many directors and editors use in chase sequences to enhance the flow of the story is to stage shots so that characters enter the frame or exit the frame. The point where the pursuer enters into shot, as the subject is on the edge of the frame, is a natural cutting point. Similarly, having the pursued exit the frame gives the editor a natural cutting point to move forward in the parallel action. It's important for the director to stage this correctly, so that if the pursuit of the action is primarily from left to right on the screen, then the subject needs to enter the frame from camera left and exit the frame on camera right. Keeping this direction correct and staging the sequence so that the editor has the opportunity to use the frame entrances or exits as cutting points will effectively enhance the drama of the scene.

The key element the editor is controlling is time. Sometimes time is being contracted, and sometimes it's being expanded. In the classic chase scene, which might start slowly, with longer shots, time might in fact be contracted. A few

Figure 9.1 Editing action

shots may show the pursuit moving over a large area and cover what may take much longer in real time than in screen time. Then as the scene develops, the pace of the cutting might get faster, while real time might be expanded. What might take only a short amount of time in real life may actually take longer in screen time to build the dramatic tension.

For the lighting director, the challenge can be even greater. While the director can fake the direction in which actors are moving as long as they are moving in the same direction relative to the camera, it's more difficult for the lighting. If the sun is coming in one direction and the director turns the scene around, the sun angle will change abruptly, upsetting the continuity of lighting. It's critical that the photographer and the director work closely to achieve the best results for continuity of action.

For the director working in conjunction with the camera operator it's important to use the composition to carry the viewer from one shot to the next. Ideally the audience's eyes will flow smoothly from one compositional arrangement to the next. Using shapes, areas of dark and light, and lines within the composition, the viewers will be taken from one shot to the next and remain engrossed without having to reorient themselves with each cut. By changing the composition between shots the viewers are given something new and remain riveted, yet the elements of each composition should guide the their eyes from one movement to the next, from one shot to the next, to give them the most engaging experience. A key ingredient to making this work is to avoid sudden changes in contrast in the sequence. Plunging viewers from darkness to bright daylight or vice versa will disorient them and break the flow of the scene. In some instances this kind of abrupt tonal change can be used effectively, but it acts as a brake, bringing the scene to a sudden halt. It should be used when the story requires the sequence to suddenly change direction or emotional tone.

Project: The Chase

This is a two-to-three-minute project designed to show off your directorial, camera, lighting, and editing skills. Working in teams of four to six you have to produce a chase or sequence. The chase may not involve any type of motorized vehicle. It requires great skill and imagination to sustain this type of sequence while keeping it dynamic. Because it's usually fast paced it requires a lot of shots, many different setups with different, interesting, dynamic camera angles.

The project can include copyright-free music and minimal dialog, but the action of the sequence should be the driving theme.

1 Begin by coming up with a concept that you turn into a presentation to the class.

2 Once the instructor has approved the concept, the team must produce either a detailed, shot-by-shot, shooting script, or a shot breakdown in storyboard form.

3 After the script or storyboard is approved, the team has to shoot the production, keeping in mind the important aspects of continuity of direction, staging, and lighting.

4 The shot material is captured and edited, making every effort to cut the action as smoothly as possible so that the continuity of action and parallel action is maintained.

5 A simple open title and closing credits should be added.

After the projects are completed they will be viewed and judged by the instructor and your classmates. The best projects will be shown to a wider audience.

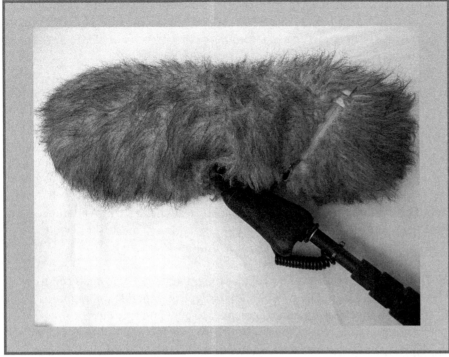

10

Sound

Audio production is key to good video productions. In fact some people say that 80 percent of good video production is good sound. The audience can accept strange lighting, unusual color balance, and special lighting effects, but unnatural or distorted sound, or muffled dialog that is hard to understand will not be accepted by your audience and is always immediately apparent.

The best way to get good sound is to get your recording microphone as close as possible to the sound source. As in lighting, the inverse square law applies equally to all radiating energy, and this goes for sound as well. Every time you double the distance between the microphone and the sound source the effective loudness of the sound is a quarter of what it was. If the microphone is mounted on the camera, the farther you move the camera away from the subject the softer the sound will become. The closer you can get the mic to the subject the better the recording will be, unless the sound is very loud, in which case getting too close to the sound source may damage the mic.

Microphones

Microphones work, as our ears do, by picking up sound waves that pass through the air, or in some cases through other conductive objects such as hard surfaces. To work effectively the mic needs to be able to respond quickly to minute changes in the air pressure caused by sound waves. Inside the mic is a sensitive coil or thin, delicate plate that moves in response to the pressure. This plate or diaphragm

Figure 10.1 Basic microphone construction. From *Audio Postproduction for Digital Video*, © 2002 Jay Rose.

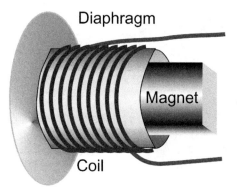

Diaphragm

Magnet

Coil

moves within a small magnetic field, which allows the movement to be translated into tiny electrical impulses (Figure 10.1). These can be amplified and recorded on magnetic tape either as an analog recording, or they be converted into digital data that's stored on tape or on a disk.

Microphones respond to sound frequencies of a very wide range. Frequencies are measured in Hertz (Hz), which is the number of cycles in the sound's wavelength per second. Good mics will respond to sound from 20Hz, which is a low, deep, bass sound, all the way to 20,000Hz, which is a high-pitched sound like the high reaches of a violin. This is pretty much the limit of most human hearing, and many microphones will have a smaller dynamic range than that, perhaps accepting sound only from 50Hz up to 15,000Hz. Though we can hear a wide range of sounds, we don't hear the whole spectrum equally well. Lower sounds are often barely audible, while higher frequencies are also attenuated, especially as you get older, or after listening to loud rock music for a while.

There are three primary types of microphones.

- **Dynamic:** This type uses a thin diaphragm attached to a small coil to pick up the sound. Figure 10.2 shows a typical dynamic microphone. The coil moves within a magnetic field to generate tiny electrical impulses. Dynamic mics are not as sensitive as other microphones but are ruggedly built and can stand some abuse. This type of mic is most commonly used by interviewers in the field. You'll see this type of mic being held up to the interviewee's mouth as they answer questions. This is the type of mic used by David Letterman when he talks to people in the audi-

Figure 10.2 Dynamic microphone

ence or on the street. What's most important when using this type of microphone is to hold it correctly. Point it at the subject's mouth at about a 30-degree angle at a distance of about 10 to 20 inches. Do not hold it directly to the mouth as this will emphasize sibilance and may make the microphone pop on plosive sounds, such as Ps and Bs.

- **Condenser:** This type of microphone uses a thin plate as a pickup. The plate itself needs to be powered to create the magnetic field that responds to the sound. This power is supplied by a small battery built into the microphone or by a battery pack that feeds power to the mic. Figure 10.3 is a typical condenser shotgun microphone with power supply. Sometimes the power can be supplied by an audio mixer that will send power to the microphone from what's referred to as a phantom power source. These mics are generally more sensitive, delicate, and responsive than dynamic mics. They are perhaps the most commonly used mic for general, high-quality sound recording.

- **Ribbon:** These are very sensitive microphones, usually used exclusively in the studio. Ribbon mics are excellent for voice recording as they produce the most accurate response to voice fluctuations. These mics are used by singers and are usually shielded by screens to prevent popping because they're so sensitive. They need to be handled with great care as they can easily be damaged, especially when put too close to loud sounds.

In addition to the way microphones pick up sound, mics are also characterized by the pattern of the direction in which they respond to sound.

Figure 10.3 Shotgun mic with power supply

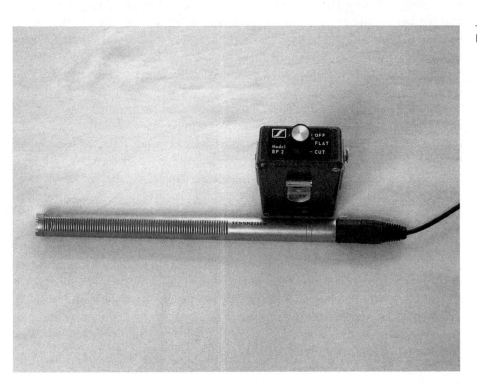

Figure 10.4 Omnidirectional microphone pickup

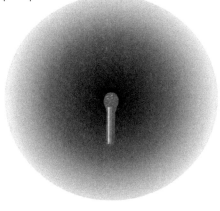

Figure 10.5 Cardioid microphone pickup

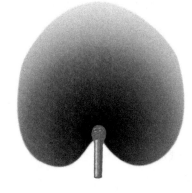

Figure 10.6 Hypercardioid microphone pickup

- **Omnidirectional:** These microphones pick up sound from all around them, pretty much equally (Figure 10.4). Despite their name they do tend to have somewhat greater sensitivity toward the front of the mic, in the direction in which it is pointed. Dynamic mics are most commonly omnidirectional and are used for general field recordings of background sounds and atmosphere. They're also used for basic interview situations, taking care to bring the mic as close to the subject as possible to separate the desired sound source from the ambient sound around it.

- **Cardioid:** These microphones pick up sound in a heart-shaped pattern, more prominently to the front and then wrapping around equally on both sides (Figure 10.5). Cardioids are used to try to isolate specific sounds. These are often condenser mics, and because they're more delicate than dynamic mics, they are usually mounted on a shock-absorbing mount so that they're not handled directly.

- **Hypercardioid:** As their name implies they are even more directional than cardioids (Figure 10.6). These mics pick up sound in a fairly narrow field in the direction in which they are pointed. Little is picked up from the sides, though some sound is picked up from directly behind the microphone. Because of the extreme directionality of these devices it's important that they be aimed carefully, directly at the sound source. If there's a little movement away from the sound, the loudness of the response will fall off quickly.

Hypercardioids are often referred to as shotgun mics, because they often are long tubes with the microphone at one end and sound baffles along their length that deaden sound coming from the sides. Some shotgun mics, which still have a cardioid pickup pattern, can be quite short, though they have still kept the name, now not so much because of their shape and size but because of their behavior. Modern shotgun mics are now often mounted on the camera, which helps to aim them toward the subject.

Lavalier mics are tiny condenser microphones that are attached to a speaker's clothing or body (Figure 10.7). They are often clipped to a lapel or onto a shirt, fairly close to the mouth. These microphones are specifically designed to be worn on a person's chest. They have reduced bass response so the lower registers do not overwhelm the microphone when they are placed against a speaker's chest cavity, which resonates with the human voice and provides most of the lower frequencies for the microphone. Because of this specific design, lavs do not work well as a mic for other uses and other sound sources.

Wireless mics are basically small, low-powered radio transmitter and receiver systems (Figure 10.8). The transmitter can be built into a special microphone, but usually is a separate box that can be used to connect most any microphone directly to a camera or to a mixer that has a corresponding receiver on the same transmission frequency. It's also common to use a wireless system to connect the sound recordist's mixer to the camera. This allows complete separation and greater freedom for both members of the team.

Figure 10.7 Lavalier mic

Figure 10.8 Wireless transmitter and receiver

Wireless mics have a limited range, sometimes no more than 50 or 100 yards in line of sight, with even more limited capabilities when there are obstructions, especially large metal objects that can act as reflective transmitters. Wireless mics are either in the VHF (very high frequency) range or the UHF (ultra high frequency) range. Generally UHF is preferred as there is less traffic on those frequencies. In populated areas there is always the danger of picking up interference from more powerful transmitters, like those in taxicab radios, using the same frequencies. Because breakup and interference is fairly common on these systems it's important that the camera operator monitor the sound that's being recorded on the camera. This is a good practice in all circumstances, even when there is a separate sound recordist and mixer. There can be a recording level problem or break-up or other interference, such as AC hum, on the connection between the mixer and the camera, so it's always a good idea to monitor the camera recording with headphones or earbuds.

Exercise: Sound Recording

This is a classroom exercise to help you to learn to listen and to try different sound recording techniques.

1 Divide the class according to the number of cameras and tripods that are available. Ideally there will be no more than four students to a camera.

2 Set up a CD player or boom box at one end of the studio or classroom and array the cameras as from the sound source as possible.

3 Distribute as many microphones of different types as are available.

4 Turn on the boom box at a moderate volume and have the cameras record short sections of sound beginning with the camera microphone.

5 Each camera should try recording the sound with each of the different mics available, with each student listening on headphones connected to the camera as the sound is recorded. As each separate recording is made, announce what mic is being used and the distance to the sound source.

6 Try recording the sound with the different mics at different distances to the sound source, getting closer and closer.

When one of the recorded tapes is played you should be able to hear the differences in acoustics and pickup of each microphone, which mic sounds more hollow and which gives better directional pickup, and which sounds cleaner and clearer the closer the mic is to the sound source.

Stereo

Most cameras' built-in mics shoot in stereo with two tracks of equal weight. That's what you usually want for scenes. You want the principal audio, like the voice of someone speaking or the sound that appears to be most important to the scene, to be coming from the center of the screen, between the speakers, where the video is. You normally do not want to hear the voice coming from two separate speakers as if there are two people speaking in unison on either side of you. Background sound is more commonly separated like this, not centered, but spread to the left and right speakers. This can be done in most editing software with a pan function.

Normally it's best to capture sound into your computer from the tape as a stereo pair, that is stereo sound centered between the speakers. If you have distinctly separate tracks on your two channels of audio, you should capture the audio as separate channel 1 and channel 2, which moves the sound to separate left and right speakers. In most editing systems you will have the option to change the sound from centered stereo to spread channels whenever you like.

Mixers

For simple location sound recording a single microphone will be sufficient, but often you'll want to have more than one mic recording the action. This is particularly true when using lavaliers, where you can have two or more mics attached to various subjects. In these instances you'll need to use a mixer to combine the sounds. The mics get fed into the mixer, which can have anywhere from two or three inputs, up to 24 in a large studio mixing console. The outputs of the mixer are fed to the camera, cameras, or deck that is actually recording the audio (Figure 10.9).

Mixers inputs are controlled with faders or gain controls, either knobs or sliders. These will allow you to adjust the input of each of the channels coming into the mixer. There will also be a master gain control, which controls the output level of the mixer.

Mixers usually have two levels of inputs and outputs. They can be either mic level or line level. This is either switchable or controlled with a knob or potentiometer, called a pot, on each channel, which gives a range of selectable levels. It's

Figure 10.9 Audio mixer

critical that the right input and output are selected. Mic level is, as its name implies, used primarily by microphones, which feed a tiny amount of sound that needs to be boosted and amplified. Cameras are designed to accept mic level at their inputs. So microphones fed into the mixer go in at mic level, and outputs being fed to cameras are set to mic level also unless this is switchable on the camera itself. Many decks on the other hand will expect audio at line level, a stronger, amplified sound that needs much lower sound levels to make a good recording. In this case the mixer outputs should be switched. Some mixers will have separate outputs for mic level and line level. It's important that the correct level is selected. A microphone fed into a line level input will produce almost no recordable audio, while a line level device fed into a mic level input will be completely distorted and can easily damage the mixer.

Most mixers have some metering device, usually VU meters (volume unit meters) to show the sound levels being recorded. Better cameras will have audio meters as well, sometimes available directly in the viewfinder or view screen while you're shooting. You should be aware that VU meters do not respond to sound instantaneously, so some sudden sounds may be above the level indicated. Some mixers will have peak program meters (PPMs), which have a much more rapid response to sound levels and are more accurate. These meters, whether VU or PPM, should be used in conjunction with the mixer pots or sliders to control the audio levels. If the sound level is too low, the pots should be turned up; if the sound is too loud, the pots should be turned down. Using the pots or sliders on the mixer, you can balance the levels between multiple sound sources, for instance between someone who's soft spoken against someone who speaks more loudly. This is one of the primary uses of the mixer.

Currently different recording devices and mixers use different "standards" for how they display good levels of recording. Analog devices, such as many mixers, will use 0dB (decibels, a unit of sound measurement) as the acceptable level for recording. Analog mixers and recording decks are said to have "headroom" that allows you to get acceptable recordings above 0dB, up to +4 and even higher without problem. Digital devices however use zero as an absolute recording level. There is no headroom and nothing above zero; at that level the sound is simply cut off and distorted, compressed down to that level. To be able to give the recording some headroom, digital devices use lower metering levels to display peak recording levels. Generally peak recording on digital devices like cameras should not exceed –12dB. On some high-end Sony decks the peak recording is even lower, set to a level of –20dB.

Normal speech should not be used as the peak recording level. On an analog device that's using 0dB and has some headroom, normal speech is recorded about –4dB, leaving space for louder transient sounds. On digital meters normal speech is usually set to around –12dB. This is generally the ideal recording level on digital meters, leaving sufficient room above that level for loud sounds. VU meters only display an average of the sound level at any moment, another reason why it's important to leave room for louder sounds, particularly on digital recording devices, to avoid distorting them. If a sound has been distorted in recording it cannot be undistorted. Reducing the level of distorted audio will simply reduce the level of distortion, but it will not remove it. If the recording is distorted it's ruined. These guidelines should be adhered to in both studio and location recording.

In addition to metering and level control, many mixers will give you frequency controls that will allow you to adjust the pitch for certain tones or a graphics equalizer to filter out specific frequencies. This can be useful if a voice is sibilant and hissy, with sharp S sounds. With careful adjustment these can be reduced. The frequency controls, usually for lows, mids, and highs, can be used to boost or reduce specific ranges of frequencies to give the voice a more pleasing tone.

Automatic Gain Control

Many cameras and camcorders have AGC, or automatic gain control. This means that the camera will automatically raise or lower the sound level to what it considers the optimal sound recording level. This can be handy for quick recordings on location without a separate mic or when shooting by yourself when you don't have enough hands to control the camera and the sound levels. In most cases on location this will work fine, but AGC is also liable to produce unpleasant pumping in the sound volume if there is too much fluctuation in the background sound. Just like auto iris and auto focus, AGC can adversely effect your recording. It's always better to switch off AGC and use a separate mixer that provides a constant sound level controlled by a sound recordist. Unfortunately, even if you are using a separate mixer and carefully controlling the levels, the feed into the camera may still be affected by the AGC function of the camera; and even more unfortunately, on many cameras switching this off is not available. On cameras that have separate audio level controls, AGC can be switched off.

When using a mixer with a camera that has audio controls, it's essential to establish a common recording level. This is usually done by generating a 1,000Hz tone from the mixer, which is fed to the camera at a specific level for calibration. On analog devices this sound level was set to 0dB; the mixer gain was set so the tone was output at 0dB while the camera recording level was set so the tone was recorded at a corresponding level. If digital recording equipment is used then the tone is set to either –12dB or –20dB. Most camcorders and digital post-production equipment use –12dB as a reference. If the mixer is an analog device outputting at 0dB and the camera uses a digital standard, the tone should be output at 0dB from the mixer and recorded at –12dB on the camcorder. It is good practice to record camera color bars together with calibration tone at the beginning of each tape.

Studio Recording

Usually studio recordings of interviews are done with lavalier microphones. Other types of dialog or performance may be recorded with mics mounted on a boom or on a desk stand. Lavs are most commonly used because they produce the best recording separation, allowing greatest control over individual levels. Because of their size, studios tend to be large, boxy rooms, often with high ceilings, all of which tend to produce a hollow, echoey sound. This is another reason lavalier mics are used, as they tend to reduce the boomy quality of many studio settings. When using multiple lavs it's essential that they be fed into a mixer. It's not a good practice to feed separate mics into separate cameras and mix them later, though this can be done. The mics are fed into a mixer, and the mixer outputs are fed equally to all recording cameras. If there are two distinct speakers, such as in an interview, what is often done is to feed both tracks separately through the mixer, and using the left and right pan functions, to send both tracks to two separate recording channels on each camera. This gives post-production the best combination of individual tracks and equal recording on all cameras.

Location Recording

Location recordings have all the problems of studio recordings without having as much control over the acoustics of the surroundings. Large rooms with bare walls and floors will have poor acoustics with a lot of reverberation and echo. In these situations it's almost always necessary to use lavalier mics to reduce the echo. If you cannot work with lavs it becomes necessary to move the mics closer to the subject than normal. This might give the sound an unnatural proximity or presence, which can be adjusted by reducing some of the bass. In some instances it may be possible to deaden poor acoustics by draping heavy blankets or putting more people or objects in the scene, or even around the room, to help to break up the reverberation.

In location recording, because there can be a good deal of unwanted background sound, it's a good idea to use mics with a cardioid pickup pattern or to use shotgun mics. These will limit the ambient sound and direct the pickup on the subject if they are properly aimed.

A great help when doing location recordings is to use a boom to which a microphone can be mounted and placed close to the subject. Special lightweight fishpoles can be used by a sound recordist to position and aim the mic toward the subject (Figure 10.10). Holding a microphone on a boom or fishpole for an extended time can be tiring and takes quite a bit of shoulder and arm strength.

In some cases microphones can be hung from boom arms or from lighting booms, though care should be taken to avoid running audio cables close to power cables to prevent picking up AC hum in the sound.

In every location—whether in the studio, on location, or outdoors—it is important to record room tone or atmosphere. Every room, location, street corner, field or forest has its own unique sound, a background, low-level sound. It's important that it be recorded with no one talking or moving about. Outdoors, where the background sound can be more variable, it's important that longer tracks with a greater variety of wild track background sounds be recorded. These are essential for post-production. Whenever the editor needs to cut out a section of sound, or spread apart some audio, if there is no room tone or atmosphere, the sound track will suddenly go dead. It is immediately apparent when this happens, and unless the editor can cobble together pieces of room tone the sound will be abrupt and jarring.

Figure 10.10 Fishpole with shotgun mic

The atmosphere recording is essential to maintain audio continuity. You want to make sure to use the same microphones whenever you record in a certain location. Mixing microphones and sound systems will produce different audio responses and when cut together will be quite noticeable, especially if there are sudden changes in the audio quality of a single voice.

Recording Outdoors

The biggest problem in location sound recording is having too much ambient noise and of course wind. Sensitive microphones pick up wind noise easily, which will ruin most recordings. When recording outdoors it's a good idea to switch on whatever wind suppression filtering may be available on your camera. This is set in a menu on most camcorders. Wind filtering can do only so much, and it is essential to have some kind of a cover or windscreen on the microphone to prevent it from having its sensitive pickup be rattled by the wind. Sometimes this can be a simple foam cover on the microphone or more elaborate plastic mesh or fiber-covered housing to protect it. Elaborate housings for microphones are also available that are excellent at suppressing wind noise. Microphone housings such as those in Figure 10.11 are often referred to as a dead cat. Sometimes a couple of layers of simple thin stocking will be enough to help reduce wind noise.

Ambient noise is best reduced by careful mic placement. Lavaliers will work well in many places to help reduce background sound. Placing mics so they are

Figure 10.11 Dead cat microphone housing

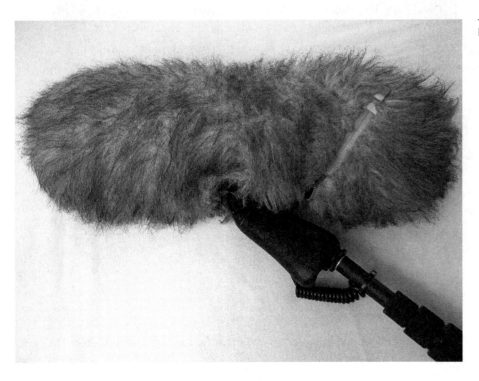

shielded from specific background sounds can help, for instance by putting your body between the mic and the direction from which the sound is coming. Or sometimes it helps to use the subject's body as a sound shield. In the studio, it's common for the microphone to be hung on a boom from above the subject, but on location the mic is susceptible to wind noise and background sounds. In these cases many sound recordists use a boom at a low angle, pointed up at the subject from below the edge of the shot.

In many instances it's important to remember that the recording of good sound outweighs the importance of getting the perfect shot. Ideally you would have both, but in many cases not everything will be under your control. Then placing the subject in a position or location that affords a good sound recording may well be more important than placing the subject where you can get the best shot. In these instances it's better to get a good recording and cover the speech with excellent B-roll, than it is to get the interview in the best location but have the sound be unintelligible.

Exercise: Scavenger Hunt   This is a timed trial to record a list of five or six sound effects which the instructor will provide. Ideally this will be a mix of indoor and outdoor sounds from a variety of accessible locations. Each group will need to record each of the listed sounds with each of the available microphones. Each recording has to be at least 20 seconds.

1 Divide the class into as small groups as possible, ideally teams of two per camera, and distribute the microphones as they are available.

2 A different sound effect will be assigned to each group to start with.

3 Each group has to go out and tape the assigned sound, first with the microphone they've been given and then with the built-in camera microphone.

4 After recording the first sound, the team returns to have the recording checked for proper levels and good sound quality. If the recording is distorted or recorded too low, the recording has to be redone.

5 After the first recording is checked, each team gets assigned a second sound effect they have to record, again with both the outboard microphone and with the built-in camera mic.

6 The first team to complete good recordings of all five or six assigned items will be the winner.

Post-Production Sound

While a lot can be done in recording to get the best possible sound, there are some things that can be done only in the editing room. This is called audio sweetening and ranges anywhere from entire dialog replacement and rebuilding of a sound design and atmosphere for a scene to simple mixing of background sounds and effects and adjusting of volumes.

Compressors

Compressors are important in post-production. They are used for a variety of types of programs. They're commonly used on music and often on narration and dialog. Compressors do what their names imply; they compress the sound, reducing the range to a narrower, consistent range of audio. The louder sounds are lower and the quieter sounds are raised. This is not the same as AGC in recording as it can be done with greater control and flexibility. Compressors do not affect all the sounds in the recording and do not shift the entire volume level up and down. They act only to reduce or amplify specific sounds that fall outside of a certain range.

In music, compressors are used to maintain the overall loudness of the track. Compressors are used heavily on commercials, which is one reason they always sound louder than the program audio. You'll also see that CD tracks when played back and monitored on your meters will appear to be at a consistent loud level, with the metering moving right up next to the threshold of 0dB. This is what a compressor does: It jams all the sound into the small range of loudness, and in the case of most music CDs, that's at absolute loudness before distortion. These levels, by the way, are too loud for use with digital video systems and should all be reduced closer to the video standard you're using, either –12dB or –20dB. Usually music should not be allowed to exceed –6dB, quite a bit lower than the original recordings.

Compressors can either be hardware devices, or more commonly, are built in as filters or plug-ins to non-linear editing software. Each piece of equipment or software will work somewhat differently, but the overall concept is that you set what you want as the peak audio and then dial in a threshold that covers a range that you want the audio to stay above in relation to that peak level. Sometimes entire programs have their audio run through a compressor, but this can produce shrill, constantly loud sound with little variation, which is probably not what you want. You most likely want some sections to be quiet and others loud. Compressors are more often used on single tracks, like a narration track. It's common for narrators to begin their first words loudly and then become softer. Compressors help to smooth out this variation, making the sound level more consistent.

Other Filters

Unlike compressors, which are sophisticated in the way they handle audio, limiters simply act to suppress audio that goes beyond a certain level. Limiters are useful in the field, where they are used to suppress sudden, loud transient sounds that might become distorted.

Expanders work the opposite of compressors and can artificially spread the loudness range of sounds that have been too heavily compressed.

Parametric or graphic equalizers allow you to emphasize and suppress specific frequencies or frequency ranges. These are useful for changing the quality of the sound, to give someone's voice more bass, or as a special effect to remove both the high and lows, or to level a narrow mid-range bandwidth, which produces a voice with a telephone effect. Like the more complex parametric equalizers, low-pass, low-shelf, high-pass and high-shelf filters will reduce specific ranges at the top or bottom end of the aural frequency range. They're commonly used to suppress background rumble in urban areas or work environments or the background sound from air conditioning systems. There are also filters for removing hum from a audio track that might be caused by electrical interference.

Most systems will provide means to add reverberation, echo or other special effects to a sound source. There is unfortunately no good way to remove unwanted echo. This needs to be suppressed during recording.

11

Dialog

*O*ne form of video production that you should try is to shoot a scene that's based on dialog. If you're working in documentary or news, this form is equally applicable to doing interviews and other staged conversations. Dialog scenes are of course key ingredients in motion pictures and any narrative fiction, short or long form. Editing action and dialog are the mainstays of narrative. In dialog, perhaps more than anywhere else, the editing happens all the way back at the writing stage. The choice of words and their order will determine the first structure of the scene. The director's choice of angles and shots to cover the dialog will be the next factor, and finally the editor will get the material, and he or she will have a selection of material. By now the order of the shots and their content will drive the editing, in both its choices and its pace.

In narrative film the choices and pacing will be based considerably on the format for which the show is intended. A theatrical release to be seen on a large cinema screen needs to give the audience more time to read the material, to see the vast scope of the content even when it's in close-up. On a small television screen the viewer can take in the whole shot immediately, without any eye movement. The pacing here might need to be quicker to maintain the audience's attention. The growing use of large-screen home theatres with close proximity seating might bring a return to a more theatrical style of editing even for home television viewing.

As we have seen in action editing, most theatrical and narrative production is based on the idea of seamless editing, disguising the cut in the action as well as in the dialog. The editor is often looking for the most natural place to cut, for the single frame that most precisely defines where an edit should take place, the moment that the great Academy Award-winning editor Walter Murch refers to as the moment the eye blinks. It's this instant, in video this 1/30th of a second, when the audience blinks because it has seen enough of a shot and is ready to move on. Murch contends that when we look from one object to another or our eyes look at different parts of the scene, we naturally blink as our eye line or head position changes. You hear the door open, and you turn to see who is entering the room. When we turn our heads, we often blink. When we're looking at the door to see who has entered, the door is already open. It is unnatural to see the door before it begins to open, though it's often used to create anticipation and suspense.

The moment the viewer's blink mechanism is triggered is to a large extent based on the shots that came before and by the sound that links the shots together. In the case of a dialog sequence, the sound is primarily the words spoken by the participants, whether actors, interviewer, or interviewee. It's their words that drive the timing of each edit and the overall pace of the scene.

In much narrative film, it's often emotion that is the key to great storytelling. Within a single scene it may be even more important than the story itself. However, for the story to be effective, it's important for the drive of the story to be maintained and not subsumed by the emotional content. Without a good story no amount of emotion will sustain the film, and it's not possible to create arbitrary numbers to measure the importance of a shot. Similarly, mechanical devices such as the line, which allow the audience to suspend belief and draw them into the reality of the story, should not be dismissed as mere props. If the audience withdraws because it's abruptly jarred by poor direction and staging, the story and its emotional drive will suffer.

Sound is the principal driving force behind the timing of edits, especially in dialog sequences. This does not always mean the edits come with the sound. They may come against the sound, and in dialog editing, most often do. You almost never slavishly cut with the person speaking; you often cut to a person after they begin speaking or more commonly before they begin to speak. It's often unnatural to cut on the gap; either you cut after the response begins, as if you're an observer reacting, or you cut while the first person is still speaking, anticipating the response.

Think of how you watch a conversation. You generally look at the speaker, perhaps occasionally glancing at the listener. When the listener interjects, you hear the voice and turn to the source of the sound. The sound comes before the picture; you hear the sound and then you see the source of the sound. Sometimes this is overt, such as the famous Hitchcock transition from a woman's mouth opening to scream, or hearing a train whistle and then seeing the rushing train. Usually the transition is considerably subtler.

In narrative film the editor often works on the assumption that the viewer grasps the situation and anticipates the response. One person speaks, and while they're talking, you cut to the other to see the reaction and anticipate the response before it begins. The second person responds, and during the response, after the subject and verb establish the sense, you cut back to the first person to await another response.

Sometimes you hold longer on the listener, especially when they're being told some piece of news that you already know. When your wife is telling a story that you've heard many times, usually you don't watch her retelling the tale; you watch her audience to see their reactions. This is especially true when someone is being told terrible news like a death in the family. If you know the news, you watch the reaction; but if it is being revealed to you for the first time, you usually watch the messenger, at least to start.

How long you hold an image on the screen is dictated by how long you want the viewer to look at it. Sometimes this is very brief. You look left and right to cross a street, and you see the two images of the street for only the briefest of moments, probably less than a second each. Often you hold on an image much longer to give the viewer a chance to look around it, to study the image. The more complex the image the longer it needs to be on the screen. The word STOP in white letters in a black background can be seen in a few frames; an Ansel Adams photograph of Yosemite's Half Dome needs to be lingered over.

There is no right way to edit any scene of dialog; no two editors will pick exactly the same frames, or perhaps even the same takes, or the same pacing, to assemble a scene.

There is a conventional pattern to structure scenes, probably still followed much of the time, and it's quite noticeable when it's not. The convention is to begin with a wide, establishing shot, and move to medium shots and to close-ups as the scene intensifies, perhaps returning to the wide shot after the climax of the scene.

Another convention is to follow your character:

1. We see the character
2. We see what the character sees
3. We see the character react

The shot progression quickly goes from wide shot to a series of singles, these singles being simple close-ups and their respective reverse angles. It is important in this structure that the characters are consistently sized on screen. It would be unsettling for the audience if the sizes of the close-ups varied greatly since we're moving from one character's point of view to the other. It's important to establish frame size for the scene so actors maintain relative size in the frame.

One of the first questions many directors and editors address when they're looking at a scene of dialog to cut is to ask themselves whose scene it is, which character is the dominant force or the one most affected by the events of the scene. This weighting of the scene will determine who is given the emphasis, whose reaction and response you're more likely to see on the screen.

In the Chapter 11 menu on your DVD is a short scene from a movie called *Heartwood*, an independent production directed by Lanny Cotler and produced by Steve Cotler, starring Hilary Swank, Eddie Mills, and the late Jason Robards. This is a short scene between Sylvia (Hilary Swank) and Frank (Eddie Mills) in which he's trying to persuade her to run away with him. The scene was shot, as is common in film production, with a single camera. Editing the scene shot with multiple cameras is somewhat easier, as in a multi-camera musical performance, but the techniques and the end result are similar. Though *Heartwood* is really Frank's movie, a coming-of-age story complicated by timber and environmental issues, the scene is more Sylvia's, I think, and Hilary Swank gives a lovely performance. If you accept the premise that it is Sylvia's scene, you should cut it so it weighs more heavily in her favor; if it's Frank's scene, it'll weigh more on his performance and on his reaction to what she says.

This scene opens as the couple comes out of an old trailer (Figure 11.1). The camera tracks slightly with them to their marks and becomes the master wide shot for the scene. The wide shot is followed by singles of Frank and Sylvia, close-ups of each of the actors' performances.

In the first cut on the DVD, the scene is done entirely conventionally; simply trading back and forth as each character speaks. Once you've worked through the lines you'll have the basic structure of the scene in close-ups, cut in its most boring, conventional manner. The audience sees who's speaking, each in turn. Despite the inconsistent dialog, the performances here are paced carefully. There is nothing worse than trying to cut together a scene in which the actors rush the performance for the takes on which they are off camera.

The second cut of the scene varies the pace and includes cutaway reaction shots of the characters during the dialog. One problem is the type of lengthy speech like Sylvia's where you might want to drop in a cutaway of Frank to see his reaction to her words. I looked through Frank's and found a reaction I liked to use (Figure 11.2). The truth is the reaction I used doesn't come quite at the moment Sylvia says her dialog, but it seems to fit nicely as a reaction to her simile about her father. I also added a couple of other cutaways, one of Sylvia when Frank says, "This is what people do." Again, the moment Sylvia's shoulders sag didn't quite come on the line, but I think it works nicely here (Figure 11.3). Using cutaways gives the audience a chance to see the other person and their response without losing the intimacy of the scene by backing out to the wide shot.

In the original film the scene was played largely in the master shot (Figure 11.4) with one close-up of Sylvia and one of Frank. It was probably right for the movie, but for this little exercise, I went for the intensity of the close-ups rather than standoffish look of the wider shot.

Figure 11.1 Establishing shot

Figure 11.2 Frank's reaction

Figure 11.3 Sylvia's reaction

Figure 11.4 Master shot

You might not have the opportunity to edit material shot by an excellent director and camera operator, with an Academy Award-winning actor and outstanding performances. If the direction, camera work, and acting aren't there, it's much harder to edit the scenes. There is only so much you can do, and sometimes no amounting of stitching will be able to make a silk purse out of a sow's ear.

Project: Dialog

In this project you will write and produce a short scene of dialog between two or three characters. The subject is open, but it should be a single scene of dialog either of your own invention or from a theatrical production. This is a two-to three-minute studio or single-location project designed to show off your camera and sound recording skills.

1 Divide the class into teams of four to seven students.

2 Brainstorm your task and come up with a concept.

3 After the concept is pitched and approved, the team should write the dialog. The script should be detailed and in feature-film script format.

4 After the script is approved the scene will be shot. It's important that the staging, camera direction, and lighting are good. Because the scene is based on dialog it is important that the sound be clear, clean, and well recorded.

5 After the scene has been shot, the project should be edited together and basic titles and credits added. Extra natural sound may be added as needed, but no special effects or transitions should be required. Your work will be evaluated by your instructor and by your classmates, and as before the best projects will be shown to as wide an audience as permitted.

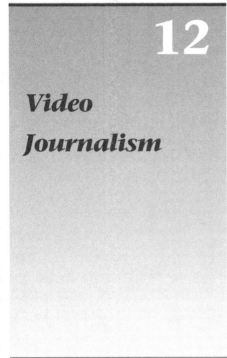

12

Video Journalism

Because video journalism is such an integral part of many school video production programs it is important to look at some of the issues it raises. Even though many of the subjects raised here are important to any video program, they are especially important in video journalism.

What Is Video Journalism?

Dictionary definitions of journalism talk about reporting, writing, photographing, and broadcasting the news. These definitions aren't really satisfactory though, as journalism, especially good journalism, goes beyond simply reporting the news. Good journalism goes beyond that and places the facts in context. A news report might say that the art department at a school is being cut back. A better report might say the cutbacks in the art department are because of budget cuts, which are due to a decline in school enrollment. A journalist might also put it in the context of diminishing budgets despite all-time highs in lottery earnings, which are supposed to help fund education.

Every day on the news, particularly on national network news, you will find most stories are placed within a wider context. Some have called journalism the first draft of history, and it's important that reports be placed within their historical context.

Journalism is immediate, so in that sense it's not history. It lacks the perspective of time. It's not always possible to foresee how important a story might be or how important it might become, or whether what seems important at first glance might dry up and be of no consequence. Without hindsight you can't tell what real importance a story might have. Some stories may start out being of only local importance, such as the disappearance of a small girl named Megan in New Jersey 10 years ago. It probably would have remained only of local interest if it had not prompted legislatures around the country to enact so-called Megan's Laws, which require that convicted sex offenders report their whereabouts to authorities who in turn have to advise local communities of the person's presence. Clearly, a reporter working on Megan's disappearance at that time could not have known the impact it would have for jurisprudence in the country. Those covering the story would be working under the pressure of deadlines that would make it difficult to foresee the outcomes. However, the coverage given the story had a profound effect on legislators, first in New Jersey and then in other states. The reportage served as a vehicle and a cause of the change that came about, altering events. To that extent journalism could be said to change history.

Journalists always have to be aware of their professional responsibilities. Whatever they write and say about a story can and often does directly affect the way the story develops. Their actions can change what happens. By focusing public awareness on a story or a situation, journalists have a much greater impact on events than most other people, and they should always be aware of how their presence and their presentation of events impact those effects and the people surrounding them.

What makes video journalism, either broadcast, cable, satellite, or even web transmission, different from other forms of journalism is that it can present motion pictures with sound of real events. In some cases it can even do it while it's happening, making the audience eyewitnesses to events. Because of its immediacy broadcast journalism puts even greater pressure on reporters than on print journalists. Trying to place a story in context during a live transmission takes not only considerable skill but also a great deal of knowledge and experience.

News

What is news? What makes one story news and another not? Basically what's news is what you think is news, or more importantly what the managing editor or executive producer of your program thinks is news. They decide what's news based on what they believe will be of interest to their audience. Some stories obviously will be of more interest to some people than to others, but whoever is making the decision about what's newsworthy needs to understanding the program's audience. They have to provide news the audience is interested in on a regular basis. If this doesn't happen, they will be replaced. So in the final analysis you could say that who decides what's news is your audience. To you what will be news is what's important to:

1 You and your family
2 Your community

3 Your country

4 Your world

For everybody the center of their news universe is themselves and their family. If something impacts you, it will be news to you. Every newsroom will see itself as the center of the world. It's no coincidence that broadcast news is centered in New York and Washington. These cities still have the largest news-gathering centers in the United States as these are the hubs of commerce and politics in our country. Local news is centered on what happens in your community. A school's newsroom, its video journalism program, will be centered on what happens in the school and also in what affects the school and its community in the broadest sense. The school community includes the larger community of parents and families and those involved in school activities within a school district. Your interest in the people and events outside your school will decrease proportionately to how far it is from your newsroom. Sometimes outside events, such as national elections or other decisions that affect your community, will come into your sphere of interest and become part of your news.

Newsworthy

What makes something newsworthy? There are no absolute rules, but there some common-sense guidelines for might be considered newsworthy.

To be worth telling a story must be informative in the sense that it tells audience something they don't already know. Too often we see stories that simply retell what's already been told and what should already be known. Avoid the type of story that regurgitates old news.

It's important for the story to be timely. News is like fish; it's good only when it's fresh, and when it's old, it smells pretty bad. If the story cannot be timely because your program is not scheduled close to the events, then try to find an angle that will make it new to the audience.

As we saw above, for a story to be newsworthy it has to be relevant to your audience. If it's not, no matter how important or how interesting to you, it probably best left out of your program. A story may be important to one audience but not to another. It's important that the stories you tell are important to your audience of viewers.

Any story that involves controversy or conflict, especially of important people, can be potentially of interest to any audience. If it is not of direct interest to your viewers, you'll have to frame the story of the conflict in a way that involves them and makes them see its significance. If you cannot do that the story will not be worth broadcasting.

In addition, any story that moves an audience on an emotional level can be newsworthy.

Finally, any story that's unusual can be interesting to any audience. Usually the story can be told briefly, but if it's entertaining and different enough it can have a place in your program. The waterskiing squirrel and the skateboarding duck are now classics of American television news. Any similar story will have a place, at least briefly, in many programs.

Objectivity and Bias

You must try to be as objective as possible when deciding what is news and what you should be covering. Try to avoid making assumptions about your audience and about what they think. When you're making a news program you are acting for your audience, so be especially careful of stories that have personal interest to you. Ask yourself if they will interest your audience as well. Working on a news program is a collaborative affair. Use that as a means of gauging your audience. Share your views with others, and respect others' views and ideas.

All news reports are biased to some extent. Liberals think the media is dominated by conservative, corporate interests; conservatives think the media is run by a cabal of left-wing liberals. Both and neither are right. We cannot help but bring our personal views to any report we do. However, no matter what your bias, it is important that you try to be as fair and objective as you can, to hide your biases so they do not color your reporting. If your bias is obvious your viewers will doubt your report. If you are perceived as having taken sides in a story, the audience will question what you have to say, and in the end you do your point of view a disservice as fewer people will be likely to accept what you're saying as true.

Types of News Stories

There are a number of different types of news stories. They all have a place in any broadcast. It's important that no single program focus on a single type of news story. If all your stories are hard news the program will seem flat. Nothing will seem particularly important because the program has no balance, nothing to counteract the hard news with something different. No single story or group of stories will stand out as more important than another. This may sound like a good thing, but in reality it's not. A show has to have ebb and flow, a rising action and a decline to a conclusion, otherwise it seems monotonous and the audience has difficulty telling what's important.

Hard News

Hard news is the most common type of news story. It's the type of story that usually headlines a program. This is a straightforward news story that presents the facts and only the facts. It's told in a straightforward manner with little embellishment or preamble: who, what, when, where, and why, usually in that order.

Hard news story are usually the most time-sensitive stories. In a campus newsroom, hard news may be hard to come by. Because of delays in broadcast and distribution much news may be dated. Nonetheless, try your best to provide some fresh news, something that's new to your audience to illuminate and explain a story. Perhaps your hard news stories will have to spend less time on the who, what, when, and where, and more on the why. In that case, so much the better. If you can explain, refine, put into context, or otherwise shed more light on a subject, then that would be your hard news story.

Issues News

This is closely related to hard news and is often also a headline story. Unlike a hard news story, an issues story tries to present opposing points of view on a particular topic or event. Usually this type of story involves some controversy or differing views of events. It's obviously a type of story most commonly associated with politics, but it does not have to be confined to politics. It can be a story about any aspect of life: academics, sports, the environment, even the staging of a play, anything that raises opposing points of views.

What's key to this type of story is that both sides be presented fairly, with no bias or point of view on the part of the reporter and the program. The story must not only be fair and objective, but it must appear to be fair. The audience should not for a moment think the story is biased. The reality of course is that in these days of political polarization, every news broadcast and news organization is perceived to be biased in one way or another. This unfortunate development has badly affected the audience's perception of the press and significantly harmed this critically important part of the American fabric. Try to go beyond these times and strive to make your stories as true, honest, and complete as you can, without bias or prejudice, untainted by favor or swayed by fortune.

Sidebars

Sidebars are stories that are related to or explain a portion of a hard news or issues story. They accompany the story and appear either in the same segment of the program or in the second segment following a break. If the sidebar is lightweight it may appear at the end of a broadcast as a show closer.

They sometimes illustrate one aspect of the story or focus on one personality in the headline story. What makes them a sidebar is that the story is linked in the broadcast and in the audience's mind with the main story. Sidebars are always related to the main story or the primary focus of a program but are tangential to it, adding more information and depth to the main story. They're not essential to the telling of the primary story or the issues involved.

Features

Feature stories are stories that are not the main focus of a program, such as human interest stories, and stories about art, science, or cultural activities. These are any stories that are not related to hard news or issues stories. Features are often "evergreen" or "shelf" stories—they are not time-sensitive and do not have to run in a particular program.

Features are often used at the end of broadcasts to close a program. They tend to be lightweight or heart-warming stories that can be used to conclude a show on a positive note. They are often humorous pieces. Over the years there have been a number of reporters, producers, and news teams who have specialized in creating this type of story, often traveling around the country to cover events and turning them into stories that serve to end programs.

Newsroom

Most video journalism programs work by setting up the classroom as a newsroom. Everywhere in the world newsrooms function pretty much the same. There are one or two people in charge, and in a class newsroom that's usually the teacher. They have the final say over who does what, how it's done, and what gets put into the broadcast. They act as the executive producer or managing editor. An executive producer, as we saw in Chapter 1, is responsible for everything in the production and for getting the program on the air. Managing editor is a position unique to news. The managing editor is responsible for the program content, decides what stories are done, and how they're done. In practice, especially in schools, the executive producer and the managing editor are the same individual.

While the teacher is in charge, the students form the production teams. Each team will need a reporter, producer, camera operator, sound recordist, and editor. Smaller teams can be used by combining jobs, but those are the primary functions that need to be done. Though some students might prefer to be reporters and others technicians, in practice it's a good idea to rotate the positions. On one production a student might be a reporter and on another would be responsible for sound. It also helps to rotate teams so that the same people don't always work together. This makes for a better program, where new and fresh ideas are coming up from different combinations of students.

Figure 12.1 The role of the reporter is to tell the story.

The Reporter

The role of the reporter is to tell the story. The reporter's job is to be fair, honest, and as accurate as possible. Given the restraints of time and technology there is only so much you can show and so much you can say, but it's important that what you do is as true to the story as it can be. It is absolutely important that you try to be as objective as possible. This can sometimes be difficult, especially if you have strong views on a subject or strong sympathy or antipathy for a subject. When your views color and affect what you have to say in a story, you're not longer reporting, you're creating propaganda.

The reporter and the producer are most responsible for a story's outcome and generally report to the executive producer or managing editor. The reporter, being the one on camera, is in the more glamorous position. There is an old adage in newsrooms that the reporters get the glory and the producers get the blame. The campus newsroom should not reflect that, and everybody involved in a story should be held accountable for its outcome.

The reporter is assisted in bringing the story to air by the producer and technicians. For a story to be successful the most important element is good communication between everyone working on the team. Everyone needs to know what the goal of the story is and to work toward that goal. All the information about the story needs to be shared with everyone on the team. The producer is the key ingredient here, and it is his or her responsibility to keep everyone on the same page and working toward the same goal. The reporter and the producer should discuss in detail with the camera operator and sound recordist not only what needs to be done but also the background to the story. They will probably be doing the primary research on developing the story, and it's important that the context of the story be passed on to the technicians by providing as much background information as possible. Knowing the context of the story lets the camera operator more easily understand what needs to be shot.

While the reporter may be assigned a story, the producer and executive producer may already have been working on it and developing it for some time, developing research, doing interviews, and developing the focus of the story. In the campus newsroom this is less likely to happen, where teams usually develop stories together. Nonetheless, in your newsroom anyone can develop, investigate, and research a story for future presentation.

Sometimes reporters write the story in collaboration with the producer, but they usually write it by themselves as it is their voice that will tell the story to the audience. In the campus newsroom the writing may be more collaborative, but remember that it's the reporter who will have to speak the words. If the reporter finds it difficult to speak the words naturally, it might be better to use other words. A stilted delivery of the narration, one which sounds as if it's being read rather than just spoken, will sound awkward.

The reporter will also be responsible for recording what's called the "on camera" or "stand-upper." In almost every story, the reporter will make an appearance, so that he or she is not simply a disembodied voice but is seen by the audience. The stand-upper is most commonly an on camera close-up, where the reporter appears at the end of the story, or as an on camera bridge, where the reporter appears in the middle of the story. Except for local news that commonly uses a donut, the reporter does not appear at the beginning of the story. In a donut the reporter, usually live on the scene, appears at the beginning and end of the story, wrapping around it, hence the name. With a few exceptions donuts are seldom used in network news and should be avoided. The strongest picture elements should be introduced first rather than the reporter.

Depending on restraints of time, stand-uppers are often written in the field and recorded on the spot while the story is being shot. This requires that the reporter have an idea how he or she will write the on camera to make it flow into the story. It can be a challenge to foresee how the on camera will fit well into the narration, but if it can be done, it provides a sense of authenticity that cannot be matched by doing the on camera in a studio or on a generic location. What is sometimes useful is to record a number of stand-ups knowing that only one will be used. This kind be time-consuming, so don't go overboard with shooting a ton of on cameras at the expense of getting the real story. Because on camera stand-ups are part of the script, they are normally approved by the managing editor before they're recorded. This isn't always possible, but in the field this is usually done by reading it to the executives over the phone. In practice for your broadcasts the on camera should probably be done without prior approval, though you should understand that this does run the risk of being rejected and having to be redone if the script does not work well with the recorded on camera. If the stand-up cannot be done on location while the story is being shot, it is also often added on afterwards, written and shot while the story is being edited. This gives the reporter the advantage of being able to add in any last-minute details.

Desk Log

Every news organization needs a way to keep track of the stories it's working on and the stories that will be coming up. There also has to be a mechanism for passing on information from day to day and from production teams to executives. In most newsrooms this is done with the desk log, sometimes called simply the log, or in some organizations the day file.

In a complex news organization each show will keep its own desk log as well as separate desk logs for different desks, one for the foreign assignment desk, one for the national assignment desk, and others for different departments. In a classroom, the log should be done by each student, every day they are in the newsroom. The log should be written up at the end of the day and given to the executive producer. This can be done on paper, on a networked computer file, or sent in via e-mail. However it's done, it should include what the student did that day, what the team did, and what still needs to be done to move the production forward.

Assignment Board

Your newsroom should have an assignment board. It's easy to make up on an erasable whiteboard. Divide the board into rows and columns. What works well is to use strips of black tape, as these should stay in place and not get erased when the board is wiped.

There should be a separate row for each production team. There can be assigned numbers or letters or colors to identify them, but if possible write the names or first names or initials of those on each team at the beginning of the row. The names are particularly important if the teams will be rotating, so everybody can keep track of who is working with who at any one time.

The columns should be divided up to cover the phases of the production process (Figure 12.1). The first column is the *Name* of each production team. The second column is the name of the *Story* they're working on. The rest of the columns cover the stages of newsgathering. The third column is usually *Research*. This can indicate what's being done, when it's being done, or a checkmark that it's been done. The fourth column is *Shot Sheet*, which is a list of the shots, interviews, locations, and B-roll that needs to be acquired to tell the story. When the shot sheet is done a checkmark can be put on the assignment board, and the team is ready to move onto the next column, *Shoot*. This might give information on when the story is being shot or that the shoot is complete; again a checkmark can be put in the column. Shoot is followed by *Script*. This indicates when the script has been written and has been approved by the executive producer. *Track* and *S/U* can either be separate columns or a single column. This would show when the script has been tracked, that the narration has been recorded, and that the stand-upper has been shot. This is followed by *Edit* and should show when the story is due to be finished. In news, especially in broadcast news, deadlines are absolute. If you don't have the story ready in time for the broadcast, it may as well not have been done. Deadlines in the newsroom should be treated the same way. They should be completely rigid and firm. When the edit is complete a checkmark can be added to the assignment board. The final column may be *Master*, which indicates when the story has been assembled into the master program reel or has been output ready for broadcast.

If you don't have enough room for all those columns, consolidate them into as many as you can accommodate.

The assignment board is there for everyone to see, so everyone can tell at any time the progress of the program and how the stories are being developed. The only person who is allowed to change anything on the assignment board is the executive producer or managing editor, or someone doing it on their behalf.

Not all stories will be needed for the same broadcast or program so it is likely that at many times different stories will be in very different stages of development. What's fairly common is to divide a large class into two groups who work on alternate broadcasts. So if you have a show scheduled once a week, one group will be working on the stories for that week while the other group will be working on stories for the program in two weeks' time. After one broadcast is complete, that group would move on to work on the broadcast in two weeks' time.

Assignment Board

Team	Story	Research	Shot Sheet	Shoot	Script	Track	S/U	Edit	Master
A									
B									
C									
D									
E									
F									
G									
H									

Figure 12.1 Sample assignment board

The groups are constantly leap-frogging each other as they prepare their programs. This can be done on one assignment board, or sometimes it's easier to have separate assignments boards, one for each upcoming program.

Programming

One of the first things you'll need to establish is how often the program will be produced. Will it be daily, weekly, biweekly, monthly, or irregular? A daily show will mean a great deal of repetitious work and will probably be best to avoid unless the school has many facilities and a large class. This type of broadcast is best for school announcements and is probably best done in conjunction with a more expanded broadcast on a regular schedule. An irregularly scheduled broadcast probably gives too much latitude without the discipline of the constraints of fixed deadlines.

Do not expect to be able to produce a full-blown program right from the beginning. It's going to take everyone time to get used to the equipment, learn the techniques, and practice them till everyone's proficient enough to get a program broadcast efficiently. In the beginning a weekly program might be more than most classes could manage, but as the school year progresses you should be able to produce excellent programming on a weekly basis, given the resources and time. You might want to start with an announcements program, perhaps only weekly, and then expand that to a fuller biweekly show that includes more complete reports, or a comprehensive monthly program that covers all aspects of the school community—academics, sports, clubs, social events, and more. Because the school schedule has times that put a lot of pressure on students, it might be better to have some flexibility when a longer program is broadcast, but do try to set a deadline for a show and stick to it. A really good, professional-looking monthly show is probably better to produce than a sloppy weekly program that looks as if it's cobbled together.

A good broadcast will include a variety of different types of stories. Some will be hard news, important pressing stories that might include issues of concern to the school community. It will also include some features, fuller stories that look at something in depth. There will also probably be sidebar stories. There should also be some reports that are lighter and more fun. A good mix of different types of stories is what you're looking to put into a program. You also would like to have stories of different length, ranging from longer features to short tells or voice-overs.

Pitching

The best way to build a program is to follow the basic principles of pre-production and production that we've already seen in the previous chapters. In the newsroom the production teams should meet to brainstorm story ideas. Each team should come up with a variety of different types of stories, probably from four to six viable stories per team.

After the ideas have been generated, the newsroom should have a pitching session. Each group should present one idea at a time, its best idea. Each suggestion should be written down, ideally on a whiteboard for everyone to see. After each of the teams has presented its first idea, the process should be repeated with a second round of stories, and then a third, and fourth round, and so on, until all the ideas have been presented. There will, in all likelihood, be some duplication of ideas, so the first team that comes up with the story, or the team with the strongest presentation or the best way of telling the story, usually gets assigned the story.

Every story proposal needs to be presented not only as an idea but also as a viable concept that can be produced by the team. The production team should be prepared to present how the story will be done, what will be shot, and show that it's feasible. Stories that are more feasible might be ones that can be shot during the class period. If that's not possible, the story will have to be shot outside of class, and that will make it more difficult to produce it well. This raises problems of coordination, transportation, timing, and permissions. That shouldn't prevent you from suggesting stories that have to be done outside of class. With a little extra effort you will be able to organize and produce excellent stories.

By going through the story ideas, the class should be able to pick out a mixture of projects, different types of news stories of different lengths that could combine well into a program that offers variety and interest to the audience. Keep stories for a news program between two and five minutes in length. Five minutes may not seem every long, but you can say a lot in that amount of time. Because you're probably not restrained by a tight program length, you can afford to produce fuller stories than is possible in a broadcast that is confined to 22:30, the length of a half-hour show without commercials. There should also be some shorter stories, from 30 seconds to a minute and a half that can be done as voiceovers or tells. These are usually read by the program anchors. We'll look at the anchors and their role in the next chapter on the studio.

Once the story selection has been done the assignment board should be updated to reflect the new assignments.

Shot Sheet

Some research will have to done before the story is pitched to make sure that it's doable, but after the stories have been approved and added to the assignment board, more research and a recce should be done.

Create a shot sheet that gives the details of shooting:

- what's the story being shot
- where the story will be shot
- when it will be shot
- who needs to be there as a subject or interviewee
- what camera, lighting, and sound equipment will be needed
- what shots needs to be taken
- what questions need to be asked

The shot sheet is usually one page long and is the primary means of communication between the members of the team. It sets out the objectives of the story and how the story will be accomplished, what's involved in producing and what needs to be done to get it on the air.

This is an exercise to produce, shoot, and edit a 30-to-40-second voice-over. This is an assigned task that will be developed into a finished project at a later date. The executive producer will have a list of short tells that need to be produced for your program. Being a kind person, the producer will let the class pick from a prepared list of assignments. If a team cannot pick one of the assigned topics, one will be assigned.

Project: The Voice-Over

1 The class should be divided into as many teams of two, three, or four as there are cameras and tripods available.

2 Each team should do research and recce the location of the voice-over.

3 Prepare a shot list of the pictures you'll need to cover the voice-over. The list of shots should be approved by the EP before you go out to shoot.

4 After the voice-over is shot, a narration should be written. Because it's a short voice-over, the narration is not recorded, but the pictures are cut to time.

5 After the exercises are completed, they will be viewed by the class. While each voice-over is being viewed, one of the team members will read the narration to check the timing with the cuts.

At a later time these voice-overs may be developed or used in a finished news broadcast.

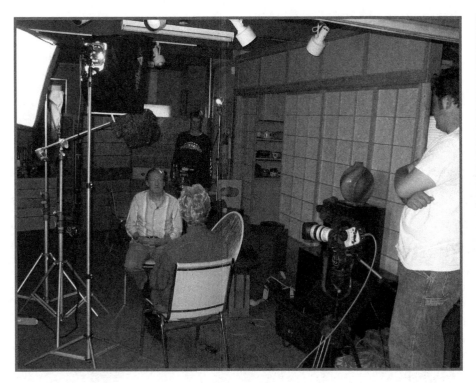

13

The News Story

This is an exercise to produce, shoot, write, and edit a news story. Together with the voice-overs done earlier, they will be used to develop a finished project.

1 The class should be divided into teams of three to five. Each team should get together and brainstorm story ideas. Each team should produce three story ideas they want to pitch and rank them in the order in which they'll be presented. Try to pick different types of stories about different subjects. In addition to the story ideas, you should also think about how you will do the story and especially consider its feasibility.

2 The class will hold a meeting in which each team will pitch one story idea in turn. The executive producer together with the class will decide if a story should be done. Once the first round of story presentations is completed, the second round of stories will be presented. Again those that are worth producing will be picked. After the third round of pitches, the final decisions will be made about who does which story. If a story has already been presented, the first pitch will be used unless the second team offers a better concept and approach to telling the story. You may not get to do a story you pitched; you may have to do a story presented by another group, but each team will be assigned a story. Unselected stories may be assigned at a later date.

Project: The News Story

3 Next each team will have to thoroughly research their story, recce any location, arrange interviews, prepare a list of questions, and put together a shot sheet of the material that you need to shoot.

4 The news story is then shot. The script is written and the pictures edited. A reporter's stand-up may be added as needed. No titles are added at this stage.

After the stories are completed, they will be viewed by the whole class and assessed. It might be possible that some of the stories will need to be reworked.

Production

Once the shot sheet has been approved by the executive producer the production team is ready to being shooting. The techniques you have learned in the previous chapters should all be used to get the best-quality video and audio, with the best lighting and sound recording possible.

Staging

When shooting material for news, it's important to understand that nothing should be staged. However, many shoots are staged to some degree, such as an interview, press conference, or photo opportunity. Though an interview is staged, the responses are not prepared in advance, rehearsed, or staged. What happens during a photo op is still subject to some spontaneity. One sharp line you should not cross is asking someone to repeat an action. At that point the scene is being staged, and staging for news coverage is never acceptable. However, if someone is going to do something, it is acceptable to ask him or her to wait before they do it to allow the camera crew to set up. That is waiting for the event to happen before it occurs; but asking them to repeat the action is considered staging. It may sound like splitting hairs, but the point is that rehearsing or telling someone how to do something is staging and should not be done. The basic rule is to cover something that would happen anyway, while making something happen is not acceptable. The dividing line can be thought to be positioning the camera and staging an event. Staging is turning reality into fiction, and the purpose of news is to as true as possible to real events.

Some events are staged, scenes such as recreations or reenactments. These are acceptable if that's the only way to tell the story, but it is important that any reenactment or staging like this be clearly indicated, usually with a title or lower-third on the picture while it's on the screen.

Camera Responsibility

The presence of the camera itself will affect a story and will inevitably serve to alter events. The camera team has an impact on what happens, but it is their responsibility to try to minimize that impact as much as possible.

This happens every day. There is a crowd protesting quietly and peaceably. The camera crew arrives, and immediately the crowd becomes more vocal, assertive, and vigorous in their protest. Quickly a small group of people becomes a forceful crowd. The presence of the camera has affected the story, changed the images, and the events themselves. It's no accident that crowds protesting in foreign countries often carry signs in English, however poorly written. The audience for the signs are not their compatriots but the cameras and viewers around the world, using the language that is closest to an international language.

The camera team should also be aware that the camera can be used to distort the truth of the image. We looked at this in Chapter 4 where we saw how the image can be distorted and how the angle affects the response of the audience. The camera can also be misleading. Again, if we look at our small group of demonstrators, if the camera shoots them with a telephoto lens, it might look like a lot of people tightly grouped together. On the other hand, shooting the same scene with a wide-angle lens, showing a small group, however vocal, with a lot of empty space around them, will have quite a different effect on the audience (Figures 13.1 and 13.2). Every shot should be considered in the light of whether it is true to the story. If you're taking pictures at a dance and there

are a few people standing around glumly, will they represent what happened at the event, or will taking shots of them be misleading? When covering an event it's important that you shoot material that actually shows what happened, and not something else, no matter how good or evocative the shot may look to the camera operator.

Camera Positioning

The way to shoot an event without staging it is to position the camera carefully, to be in a place where you can cover the event unobtrusively and still be able to capture what happens with a minimum amount of effort and little movement of the camera. A classic example is shooting a long line of people, like a row of soldiers. If the camera is directly opposite the line, the only way to see them all is to use a wide shot, in which case they will be very small in the frame, or to pan along the line from one end to the other, a long, probably slow move. Better would be to look at the line of soldiers from an angle. Now the camera does not have to be as wide to see them all, nor does it have to pan as far to go down the line. Shooting something symmetrically is pretty boring anyway; shooting at an angle almost always looks more interesting and dynamic as it creates a diagonal across the frame.

When covering an event it's important to think ahead of time about what shots you need to tell the story. You'll need a variety of shots—long shots, medium shots, and close-ups. But with the camera positioned too close you won't be able to get long shots without moving the camera farther away; positioned too far away and you can't get good close-ups; somewhere in between usually works best.

If the sound is important and the microphone is mounted on the camera, it has to be close to the subject or it will not pick up the necessary sound. For an interview in a noisy area, that means shooting a close-up with the camera probably closer to the subject than the camera operator or the subject would prefer. A better position would be to use a wireless mic that lets the camera be farther back from the subject.

If you have you have to shoot without a tripod, try to shoot with a wide-angle setting on your zoom lens. It will make the shot easier to hold steady. On a telephoto setting, even a small movement will appear as a jerky image. When shooting with a wide-angle lens it's important to get close to the subject so you get close-ups. Though it may seem a bit intrusive, in these circumstances it's often necessary to get a good picture. Try to balance the importance of getting the right shot with being too intrusive to the point of affecting the scene and the subjects.

Though you may get a majority of your shots from one good position, try to move about to get a variety of shots from different angles, bearing in mind the Rule of the Line. Sometimes it's necessary, but try not to do it if it's at all avoidable.

Cutaways

You can never shoot too many cutaways. Your editor will always thank you for them. Something to cut to that is away from the main action but within the con-

Figure 7.2 Student interview

text of the scene is always useful. This is the shot of the crowd watching the game, the shot of the interviewer listening to the interviewee, the shot of someone doing something away from the action. These are shots that can be used pretty much anywhere in the story or the interview and allow the editor to bridge one goal being scored to another, or a break in the speech, or some change of scene. Cutaways are used to cover jump cuts as we saw in Chapter 2. It's important that the camera crew shoot enough of these to allow the editor to smoothly edit the scene together.

Interviews

Interviews are usually an essential part of any news story (Figure 7.2). These can be with anyone involved in the story or with an expert on a related topic. Interview subjects can be eyewitnesses, someone who took part in an event, experts on a subject, or commentators in a particular field.

Good interviewing takes practice and skill, but there are some techniques that will make it easier.

One of the first things to decide is who you want to interview. Usually the most obvious choice is the person who was there or who knows about the subject. Sometimes that person isn't available, does not want to be interviewed, or has a terrible stutter or something else which will completely distract the audience. Forcing someone who can't speak well to appear on camera is often counterproductive. In these cases it's better to get someone who can speak well and appear acceptable on camera. A good secondary interview will almost always serve the story better than a poor primary interview. What many producers do is to interview both subjects, perhaps using the poor primary interviewee briefly to show his or her presence, while relying on the secondary subject for the bulk of the interview content.

Whenever you arrange an interview, tell the subject the purpose of the interview. Be honest with them. Never try to mislead or misrepresent why they are being interviewed. Also make sure they understand what's involved in doing the interview, how long it's going to take, how many people will be there with what kind of equipment. Also make sure they understand what kind of space is needed and don't underestimate how long it will take. It always takes longer than you think to find the right spot, set up the equipment, light the scene, and set the sound equipment, do the interview and extra cutaways and questions, and then finally break it all down. There are always snags that come up along the way, so allow more time than you think you'll need. Small delays can add up.

Interviews are shot first. While the interview is being done the producer and the production team should be making notes about what's being said and about what possible B-roll you might need to get to cover portions of the interview, or pictures you can shoot that would reaffirm or dispute what the interviewee is saying.

Let's start by looking at different types of interviews and what the differences mean in practice.

Types of Interviews

Interviews can be broken down into four types:

- the reporter interview
- the producer interview
- the sound-bite interview
- the narration interview

Each of these types of interview requires slightly different techniques for production.

In the reporter interview, the reporter is heard and sometimes even seen. This is a two-person interview that allows you to cut to the interviewer.

In the producer interview, the questioner is neither heard nor seen. In many cases the interviewer does not even wear a microphone, so that there is no chance that his or her sound will interfere with the interviewee's answers. This type of interview is harder to produce than a reporter interview, as it requires that the interviewee be made to answer fully and concisely in sentences that can easily be used in editing. In the two-person interview you can always cut away to the reporter, but in a producer interview this is not an option. The producer interview is usually shot with the intention of covering portions of it with B-roll. It also assumes that there will be a reporter or narrator who can lead into the answers, often providing the questions that were asked by the unseen producer.

Many interviews are shot to provide a single sound bite often a response or reaction to something. In this type of interview, which can be done by either a reporter, producer, or production assistant, the goal is to get a single sentence or phrase. A full interview is not necessary nor the intent of this type of interview, so it is important to focus on getting the right response to the right question. Sound bites are from about eight seconds, up to 20 or 30 seconds, which would be quite a long bite. If the sound bites are longer, it might be better to split them up or to cover them, at least partially, with B-roll. Unless it's extremely compelling watching someone speak for 20 or more seconds is enough to make your audience's attention wander off.

Another type of interview, which is similar to a producer interview, is a narration interview. The purpose of this type of interview is to use most of the interview to provide the bed for the story. The interviewee's sound will be largely covered with video, but unlike a producer interview it does not rely on a reporter or narrator to provide the lead-in or link to the questions. The interview itself becomes the sole source of narration. Often a number of these types of narration interviews are pieced together to form a single, continuous sound track. Many times these narratives might be contradictory or provide different points of view, but together they form a whole that is used as the basis for the story. Different stations and networks will have different terms for this type of a story, but they all come down to the same thing, and if done well they can be a powerful storytelling device.

In most of these types of interview, even a reporter interview, the interview is shot with a single camera, but occasionally a reporter interview will be shot with multiple cameras for convenience and ease of editing. First the camera is pointed at the interviewee to shoot the subject's answers as they respond to the questions. Then the camera is turned, or the interviewer repositioned, to shoot the questions being asked. It is absolutely important that you ask the questions in the interview shots exactly as they were asked during the interview itself. It is essential that you be true to the original event and not try to color or rephrase the question to change the shape or context of the interview. This is quite unethical and should never be done. While the reporter is being shot it is common practice to shoot some material of him or her as if listening or reacting to the answers. Again every effort should be made not to do anything that would color the audience's view of the answer. In many news organizations the reporter is not even allowed to nod to a response, as this would indicate affirmation or agreement. The reporter does not smile or laugh unless there is something obviously humorous in the answers. It is important the reporter appear as neutral and evenhanded as possible in response to interviewee's answers.

Interview Basics

The most important skill the interviewer needs to master is preparation. Know what you're asking about as well as you can, whatever the subject. Do research and find out as much as you can about who you're interviewing and the subject you want to talk about. Use all the research tools you have available on a subject: the Internet, books, newspapers, magazines, other video reports.

If you are prepared you will probably have a fairly good idea what the interviewee will say. Your job as the interviewer is to get them to say what they're going to say in a form that's useable in your program. That means the subject needs to answer, clearly, succinctly, and completely. If you know the gist of what the interviewee will say, prepare questions that will make them say that. Write down the questions on 5×4 cards or in a notebook. Try to think up five good questions that you want to interviewee to answer. Once you have the questions, think of what would be the best order to ask them, progressing from simpler questions to more complex ones.

Before any interview make sure you contact the interviewee to confirm the time and location of the interview to at least you remind them and perhaps get them thinking about what they will say. Make sure you arrive on time. It's better to be early than to be late. If you will be late, or if the interview has to be postponed or cancelled, make sure you tell the subject as soon as possible.

It's good practice to begin every interview by asking the subject his or her name and asking for the spelling as well as their job title or function, if this isn't obvious. This is done with the camera rolling. It helps to set the subject at ease, and more importantly it identifies the interview so that the correct lower third with name and title can be created in post-production. It's also useful for the reporter when the lead-in to the interview or sound bite needs to be written. Follow this up with a few easy questions. As the subject settles down and gets more and more comfortable with the camera you can add more probing and difficult questions.

When you're preparing your questions it's important that the questions are phrased so that they have to be answered fully. Never ask a question that can be answered with a yes or no. If it can be, it will be. Also avoid questions that can be answered with a single word, like what is your favorite color, or how old are you. These are fine as preliminary questions that you don't really intend to use, but for most situations you'll want a fuller answer that can be easily used in your story.

It's important for the questioner while doing the interview to not only ask the questions but also to listen carefully to the answers. Don't start thinking about your next question while the interviewee is answering. Listen to what they're saying as you may have a follow-up question, or a question that you were planning to ask later might be more appropriate because of what the subject just said.

Do not hurry the interviewee. Wait for the subject to answer the question, and then wait a bit longer. Don't rush right into the next question, even if it's an obvious follow-up. If nothing else the little pause will make it easier for the editor to get in and out of the answer without clipping your words. Also, pausing after the question encourages the interviewee to continue, to amplify and expound on what they were saying. Nature abhors a vacuum, and people tend to abhor the silences in a conversation and tend to fill them by speaking. By pausing you're encouraging the interviewee to fill the silence. Be careful though that the interviewee doesn't wander off topic. Try to bring them back on track as quickly as you can.

Camera Position

Positioning the camera is key to a successful, well-shot interview. The camera is placed behind the interviewer and slightly to the side so that it can look over his or her shoulder. Make sure the camera isn't too close to the shoulder in case the interviewer moves slightly and obstructs your view of the subject. The interviewer should remind the subject to look at them at all times and not to the camera.

The closer you can get the camera to the interviewer's shoulder the more it will be looking straight at the interviewee's face. Here's the problem: the closer it is to the direct eyeline of the subject the more likely it is that he or she will glance away from interviewer and take a peek at the camera. This furtive glancing at the camera looks unnatural and breaks the setting of the interview for the audience. The farther the camera is from the interviewer's shoulder, the greater the angle at which you're looking at the subject, the less likely it becomes that this will happen. When you reach the point that the interviewee actually has to turn his or her head to see the camera, then it becomes unlikely they will do that. You can move the camera out from the interviewee's eyeline by about 30 to 40 degrees, which should be enough. The more someone is accustomed to being interviewed on camera the closer you can bring the camera to the eyeline without danger of them glancing at the lens. Try to keep the camera in a position where it can see both eyes of the subject, not so far at an angle that only one is visible to the audience. Inexperienced people and children in particular are more prone to this. When interviewing small children it's often necessary to shoot them in profile to get them to stop turning to the lens. Unfortunately this means you'll only see one of the child's eyes, but it's the price you have to pay.

The camera should be placed at eye level of the subject or slightly below. If the person is seated, that means lowering the camera. If the subject is a small child that means handholding the camera and sitting, kneeling or squatting down. In Chapter 5 on camera shots we looked at the impact on the audience of high and low camera angles. During an interview you never want the camera position to color the audience's perception of the subject.

Sound

Sound is the critical element in most interviews. If the audience can't understand or hear the sound the interview has no value. The sound is more crucial than the picture. It's better to place the interview in a location that allows for decent sound recording than in a spot that will give the best picture. It's the production team's obligation to weigh the needs of both picture and sound and to find the best compromise that will give the best results for both the camera operator and the sound recordist.

The goal of the sound recordist is to getting the clearest, cleanest recording possible. This means separate the interviewee's speech from the background sound as much as possible. Whenever there is loud background sound position the interviewee with a lavalier microphone with his or her back to the sound source. The body will act as a shield to reduce the background sound. If a lavalier mic is not available, use a shotgun mic to reduce the ambient sound. Usually you don't want to see the mic in the shot, but if the background is very loud, such as in the stands or the sidelines of a football game, bring the microphone as close to the subject's mouth as you can and use a foam cover.

Scripting

Once the interviews have been done and the B-roll shot, it's time to write the story. It's much like writing a documentary—you're looking for the best way to tell your story with the material you have on hand.

News stories are written in the two-column format that we saw in Chapter 6 on pre-production. The narration and the sound from the interviews goes in the right-hand column, and the pictures and other graphical elements go in the left-hand column. The picture information goes parallel with the text, a brief description of the B-roll shots that correspond with the script narration.

Writing the News Story

A good starting point is to look through your interviews and pick out the sound bites you want to use. Then write the lead-ins to the sound bites, what you will say to introduce the person. The lead-in is often a paraphrase of the question that was asked. Do not ever write a lead-in that says the same thing that the interviewee says. Do not write: "The coach told us basketball is played with a round ball," when the next words the audience hears are the coach saying: "Basketball is played with a round ball." Better to say: "The coach told us about the fundamentals of the game."

Next look for your strongest picture. You want the strongest image and the sharpest words to draw your audience into the story and make them want to watch. That striking picture together with what's important in the story is your opening. Try to find a clever or intriguing way to phrase that opening sentence. If you do you've got your audience hooked.

The last part is to link all the pieces—your opening, lead-ins, interviews, and a reiteration at the end about why the story is important. There is an old adage in news reporting about writing for your audience: You have to tell them what you're going to say, you have to tell them the story, and then you have to tell them what you told them. These three make up the story: the opening, the body, and the close.

Your story is like an essay, but remember that you're not writing an essay. You're only writing the pieces that link the elements of the essay, the pictures, sound bites, and on-camera appearances. Short declarative sentences have more impact for an audience that's listening than long sentences with sub-clauses. If the audience gets lost in your train of thought in a convoluted sentence with modifiers and tangential asides, they will lose interest in the story. The narration should complement, not describe what's in the pictures. Avoid telling the audience what they're seeing unless the picture is unclear or confusing.

Stand-ups

Stand-ups or stand-uppers are on-camera appearances by the reporter where he or she speaks directly to the audience. These are most commonly done as stand-up closes at the end of the story. They're sometimes done as a stand-up bridge in the middle of a story, and rarely as a stand-up open. The stand-up open is common in local news reports, where it's done as part of a donut. The stand-up open will be live, followed with the taped report, and concluded with a live stand-up close. The package of opening, taped piece, and close is known as a donut.

Wherever the stand-up appears it serves a few useful purposes. It shows the reporter, so that he or she is not an unseen, disembodied narrator. It involves the audience in the story and shows the reporter's participation in the events the audience is watching. Stand-ups are often used to tell the audience a piece of information for which there is no B-roll picture. They are also used as a bridge between two separate parts of a story, serving as a useful break that divides the piece. As a stand-up close they are most often used to update the story or put in some late-developing information.

Stand-ups are often shot on location while the story is being shot. This requires the production team to have a good idea where the script is going and how the stand-up will be used in it. It is also common to shoot the stand-up while the story is being edited. This leaves the production team with the opportunity to add in information that was missed or to update it with last-minute information. Make the stand-up location reflect the story, even if it's as generic as shooting it in front of a tree for an environmental story or in front of a bank for an economic story. Sometimes stand-ups are done in the studio, but it's better do them on a location that is appropriate to the story you're doing.

Never begin a stand-up with the phrase: "I am standing here...." The audience can see that you're standing, and if the shot is well-composed and framed they can also see where you're standing. Sometimes a reporter might say: "Behind me you can see..." which should only be used if it's not clear what it is that's behind the reporter. The stand-up is a key element in your script, so it should be well-written, direct, and as compelling as you can make it.

Post-Production

One of the hallmarks of news production is the severe time constraints that are put on the production team. Speed in every step of the process, especially editing, is critical. Absolute deadlines and limited time make for great pressure and require great skill and experience to execute well. Hopefully your news production will not be under these kinds of time pressures. Nonetheless, you will probably have fixed deadlines.

Editing

In normal production the first steps of editing are to log your material—to go through it, make notes about the content and the pieces you want to capture and those you won't need. In news editing which doesn't have this luxury of time and is usually working with less material, everything gets captured and sorted out, discarded or saved, right in the non-linear editing system where it can be done much more quickly. The sound bites that work are pulled out of the interview and arranged in the order in which they'll be used. The shots are edited down so that you have rough selects of the B-roll material you want to use in the finished piece. Leave these long. Do not trim them too tightly at this stage.

Next the narration is recorded. There will probably be some stumbles and bad takes. Cut these out and put the good takes in between the selected sound bites in the order laid out in the script. Usually the narration is laid on a lower track, leaving the primary tracks free for interview sound and for the background sound that goes with the picture. Your editing system should be able to designate which sounds are edited onto which tracks. You can often extend an interview in the front so that the introduction or lead-in is over the picture, with the interview sound down low, and when the lead-in ends, bring up the interview sound to full level. This is called backtiming and is easy to do on most multitrack, non-linear editing systems. This will provide the bed for your edited piece. Finish this by adding the B-roll in the areas with no picture and over any interviews and on-cameras that you want to cover.

What often works well is to have the on-cameras or interviews slightly overlapped. Perhaps the reporter or the interviewee begins speaking while we still see the previous B-roll before we first see the person speaking. You can begin a piece with natural sound rather than narration. If you have a good, strong piece of sound, like a band playing or a crowd cheering, the picture and natural sound will often make a strong opening. Follow it with an interesting or intriguing opening line, and you'll have your audience hooked.

The audience cannot see and listen at the same time. They will either watch the picture or they will listen to what you're saying, seldom both. If the picture is strong, let the picture run, at least for a short time, without any narration. Open the track up and slide everything down to allow the audience a moment or two to see and understand the picture before the narrator's voice is heard. The more powerful the picture the more necessary this becomes. Cut the narration so that the reporter speaks around the picture and always over it. If it's a well-written script that complements rather than describes the picture, it should serve to provide additional information for the audience related to the pictures they're seeing.

When the B-roll becomes so mundane that it serves little purpose in moving the story forward, it's called wallpaper. Many news stories have a good deal of wallpaper in them, generic or repeated shots, or pictures the audience is long familiar with. These serve little purpose except as a vehicle to fill space for the narration to be heard. Avoid using wallpaper. Hopefully the crew has provided striking images and compelling video that drives the narration forward.

Finally the stand-up close is added on, and the graphical elements such as lower-third identifiers put over the picture. On stories that do not have accessible B-roll, much of the video information will be made up of graphics, still images, maps, animated text, sometimes even 3D animations to explain complex events. These are all created in specialist software applications. If you have access to this kind of software you should take advantage of these tools to incorporate this kind of visual stimulation to your piece. Often good graphical elements with animation and interesting, creative treatments will be much more effective that poor B-roll wallpaper.

Editing Ethics

Just as in shooting there are ethical judgments based on honesty and respect that have to be made in the editing room as well as in the field. This is especially true when using reaction shots. You should avoid significant reactions that would tend to color your audience's reaction to a person, what they're saying, or to an event that's happening.

Editing is based on decisions about what to put in and what to leave out. Do not leave out important elements or put in misleading elements, both of which might change the audience's perception of events. You have to be true to the story you're telling and in a larger sense to be honest to the reality of the events in your story.

You should not include misleading material. Avoid using pictures that are not of the real events you're portraying. If you have to use archival footage or something similar, make sure they are clearly labeled with graphics that say exactly what the elements are.

Program Formats

The structures of regularly schedule broadcasts, particularly news broadcasts, tend to follow set formats. Every show creates its own formula for its structure. There are tried and true formats.

For news programs the formula is to begin with a headline story, the most important news story or the strongest story you have. The headline story is often followed by a sidebar. These stories will make up what is called the A block, which is the first segment of a program before the first commercial break. Your programs probably won't have commercial breaks. Nonetheless it's probably a good idea to do something to break up a program into segments, to tell the audience that one set of related stories are over and that the program is moving on. A simple animation or graphical treatment with a short musical sting is often enough, an event that's programmed into a show that an audience learns signals the end of one segment and the beginning of another.

The A block is followed by the B block, which usually contains secondary news stories or features, minor hard or issues news stories. The B block is made up of shorter stories or voice-overs in which the anchor reads over some B-roll that illustrates the story. If there are no relevant pictures the anchor reads the story with some graphical treatment or a still image over his or her shoulder. The shot is framed to accommodate the graphic and is added live or in post-production. We'll look at anchors and program assembly in more detail in the next chapter.

The C block or third segment of a broadcast is used for longer feature stories. Occasionally it's used for a longer hard news or issues story or even a sidebar. The third block tends to be used for longer stories that need more time to explain the events or issues fully. They often fill the entire segment.

The final segment of a broadcast is reserved for lighter, frivolous, or emotional and uplifting stories. It's always a good idea to end a program on a positive or lighthearted note rather than to leave your audience with a downer.

When you're making up your show lineup it's better to break up groups of long stories with shorter stories. It's not a good idea to have a group of long stories together, followed by another group of short stories and voice-overs, though you'll often find this as characteristic of the B block.

These are suggestions of a typical program format, but there are no hard and fast rules. Over the years many different formats have been tried, used for a while, and then changed. Whatever format you choose to use, understand that formats create expectations in viewers and give them guidance about what's significant and important. The format also serves to give a program structure, such as when it creates a strong opening, has interest in the middle, and then lets the audience down lightly, a three-act drama.

Because most television programs have fixed formats, that does not mean you have to. You are free to try any format you like as long as it works and remains honest and true to the stories you have to tell.

The program lineup is usually created first by the line producer in conjunction with or with the approval of the executive producer and managing editor. The line producer is the one in charge of a specific broadcast. This is often used on shows where multiple line producers will be working on programs days or even weeks in advance. Usually line producers and their teams work in leapfrog fashion, giving each team more time to produce its broadcast.

A good show lineup flows naturally from one topic to another. The main story is naturally followed by related stories, which lead us inevitably to the stories that follow and have an appropriate show ending. Writing that links the segments and stories in the program, will go a long way toward making a good lineup seem great, perhaps better than it actually is on paper. Well-written intros, story introductions, and even more importantly, well-written outros, that come out of one story and cleverly segue into another topic are priceless. Segues that connect segments into a whole broadcast, and anchors who can deliver the links well go a long way to enhancing your show. Often though there is no good way or neat turn of phrase to take you from one subject to another, and here simple devices are used. Sometimes the device is as simple has having the anchor turn from one camera to another. This simple movement, together with the shot change, acts as punctuation to the broadcast. Sometimes the device used is changing from one anchor to another. Other times it might be some graphical or animated treatment that tells the audience the show is moving on to something new.

This is a final news project that assembles the voice-over and news stories that have already been produced.

Project: The News Program

1 The executive producer together with the class will decide the formatting for the show and the order in which the stories and voice-overs will be presented.

2 As no anchors have probably yet been created for the newsroom (we'll look at that in the next chapter), the EP together with class will decide who will be the voices of the program, the off-camera anchors who will lead and close the show as well as narrate the voice-overs.

3 The voice-over portions of the program will be tracked and the program assembled.

4 Finally graphics, including an opening title sequence, developed by you using a consistent style will be added to the whole program.

Once the program is assembled it will be broadcast and distributed to the widest audience possible.

In a video journalism program this process of program production will be used again and again to create shows for broadcast. In all likelihood you'll want to add anchor presenters into the mix to give students an on-air presence as described in the next chapter.

The Studio

In Chapter 8 on lighting we looked at some of the technical aspects of studio creation and work. In this chapter we're going to look at studio operations and the role of studio anchors in the campus productions. For 50 years the concept of the anchor as the pivotal role in news production has been established. The anchor is obviously a key ingredient in a video journalism or school reporting program, but less obviously the anchor or anchors are important to many other types of programming: interview shows, sports programming, and many reality and documentary programming, where the reporter or narrator can be considered the anchor.

Anchors

Anchor is probably not a good term for this function, as it doesn't so much weigh down a show (or hopefully doesn't) but rather acts as the mortar that holds the show together. I suppose "mortar" isn't quite as catchy as "anchor," but without the mortar the structure of the broadcast would crumble into separate blocks and never make up a whole. It's what gives the structure substance. Anchors bind the elements of the program together. They serve to set the tone of the program, its character and its personality. They are the visible face of the program, the audience's guide and someone with whom the audience feels a personal relationship.

The importance of the anchor as the projection of the program onto the audience cannot be overestimated. The audience's response, whether it's good or bad, creates a personal, almost intimate bond with the anchor. This bond is crucial to the success and acceptance of a show. If they are not people the audience can feel comfortable with, the chances of the program being successful is greatly reduced.

Perhaps even more important for a broadcast that's seen beyond the campus itself is how the wider audience receives the anchors. They then act not only as the face of the broadcast but also the face of the whole school program, the district, and the broad school community of students, teachers, administrators, staff, and parents. The audience will always associate the presence of the anchors in a broadcast as significant representations of your school and everyone involved in it. This is a great responsibility and not one to ever be taken lightly.

There are a number of elements that are critical to an anchor's presence. Perhaps the most critical aspect is speech. Anchors need to speak clearly, with good diction that enunciates words correctly, is easy to understand, and is as free as possible of slang. Part of this of course is the writing, but a major part of it is the delivery. No matter how carefully crafted the words, if the delivery is slurred, halting, rushed, or garbled in any way, the audience will have difficulty understanding and won't feel comfortable with the anchor.

The quality of the voice is another key element. A voice that grates or is difficult to listen to will soon be tuned out. Different nationalities have different expectations of what a pleasing voice is, what's pleasing in a male voice and what's pleasing in a female voice. In the United States we expect the female voice to have a higher pitch than a male voice. So a pair of anchors with a high-pitched male voice and a deep female voice might grate on an audience's ears. A neutral, pleasing, accent-free voice has become the norm in America. Even in areas of the country with distinct speaking and pronunciation patterns, the voices of the anchors are expected to be neutral in coloration and free of quirks of accent.

Anchors are good readers. Being able to read fluently, without hesitation or stumbling, is an important job requirement. Almost everything an anchor says is read off a teleprompter during the recording or broadcast of the program. A teleprompter is a television screen mounted under the camera lens with a one-way mirror that's angled to reflect the screen to the anchor. The camera can look through the glass with minimal light loss, while the anchor looking at the camera sees only the reflection of the script that's displayed on the screen. The text is made to move across the screen so the anchor can read from it continuously without pausing. Simple, easy-to-use, affordable teleprompters are available and should be used whenever possible. Many prompters are portable and can be quickly and easily mounted in front of a camera with the right support and can be used on location.

Except in unusual circumstances, when there is breaking news that requires a change in the program, this is the operating procedure for every anchor or presenter anywhere in the world, local, national, or international.

Though anchors read from a teleprompter, they still have printed scripts at hand in case there is a problem with the prompter and to give them something to do in those momentary pauses when changing from one story to another. It's common to see anchors looking down and rearranging their papers before beginning with a new subject.

The ability to read clearly, with, awareness and composure, is important, even when reading something you've read only once a short time before. An anchor has to be able to read while pretending not to be reading, as though they were speaking to a friend. A good anchor can read almost anything, even a telephone book, and make it sound interesting.

Another important element is clothing. As mundane as this may sound, it is essential that the anchor's clothes be suitable and respectful of the audience. Sloppy or dirty clothing, or T-shirts with large, distracting words or logos should be avoided. The audience would not be watching and listening to the anchors but reading what's on their chests. Anchors should always be neatly dressed when they're on camera. They should wear light-colored or pastel shirts or blouses, never white. Pure white is usually too bright for television. Bright colors, especially reds, yellows, and oranges, often bleed in the video signal, smearing the image and running into adjacent colors. These should be avoided in favor of more muted colors. The focus should be on the anchors and not on their clothing. The anchor's appearance, clothing, hair, makeup, and bearing affect how he or she is perceived and accepted by the audience.

Finally, appearance is important. As crass as this may sound, good-looking people are easier to watch than unattractive people. Not that being an anchor should be a beauty contest, though sometimes in America it seems to have gone that far. It is better to be more normal and natural-looking rather than a great beauty. Anchors who are pleasant in appearance and have a natural, relaxed manner will be effective. Anchors, however gorgeous and handsome, who look and act ill at ease in front of the camera as if they were deer caught in the headlights will serve you less well.

The key to success as an anchor is the same ability that's needed to be successful as an actor. If you can pretend to be sincere, you can be successful. That's harder than it sounds, and it's a difficult quality to assess, but it's a judgment your audience will make after seeing and hearing you for the first time. You will be assessed based on your appearance and on your personality. You will be judged on whether you are warm and friendly or cool and aloof. You will be judged on your trustworthiness, whether you seem honest, forthright, and sincere. Your personality will very much determine how the whole program is judged.

Though all of these elements are critical for anchors, they are equally important for anyone who appears on camera, whether in the studio or in the field, whether a reporter or narrator who's a significant presence in a project, or even someone who briefly appears as an interviewer. They all can be considered representatives of your school community to a wider audience. They should all be held to the same high standards of behavior and appearance.

Everyone who works in the campus newsroom has to be aware of this constantly, aware of how they look and behave, and how what they write, say, and do will reflect their school community to a wider audience.

Exercise: Anchor Tryouts

This is less an exercise than a process of selecting a number of students who can be anchors for your programs, news, sports, or other studio and live events. All the students in the class should do this, whether they really want to be considered as anchors or not.

1 Each student should prepare a short intro script or use a voice-over script.

2 Next the students should tape each other reading a couple of different scripts in the anchor set. Use a teleprompter if possible.

3 Once everybody has been taped, review the tapes with the whole class to see who works for your program. Select a group of students so you're not relying on just two or three.

Studio Options

A school's studio operations have a number of different variables, options that might be used for your productions. You might wish to start with one of the simpler options and move on to more complex operations. What determines which option your school chooses is based partially on equipment funding, how much equipment you can afford, and on the size and capabilities of your class.

The format you broadcast your program in is another key component. If you have no live broadcast capabilities, for instance if your studio isn't wired into a distribution channel, then a live broadcast is obviously an option. For most any live broadcasting option some kind of video and audio switching needs to be available.

There are five primary options to choose from. Each is based on some degree of studio production. The more that gets done within the studio, the less that has to be done afterwards. If little is done in the studio, more will have to be done on tape or in post-production. If everything is done in the studio, you will finish with a complete production.

Camera Taping

In this option one or two anchors are taped in the studio. More than one camera can be used, but the purpose is to get the anchor portions of the program on tape. The recordings of their portions of the broadcast, spot intros, voice-overs, and interactions are edited into the final program. The anchor tapings are captured into your non-linear editing system and strung together with your edited pieces. Any additional graphics, such as program opens, lower-thirds, and over-the-shoulder graphics can be added at this point. If you want to add graphics behind or around the anchors, you have to be careful to shoot them either framed properly to allow space for the graphic or against a greenscreen that can be keyed out and replaced.

Once the program is edited a master reel is created, which can be broadcast or distributed in other forms such as VHS, online, or on disc.

Switched Taping

This is a significant variation of camera taping. Here the studio is set up with a video switcher and cameras controlled by a director. Here the anchors are recorded live to tape, and cutting between the cameras is recorded through the switcher onto tape.

After the studio recording, the material is captured and edited into the final broadcast. The program can be simply assembled, as the anchor lead-ins are self-contained, do not need further editing, and can easily be dropped in between the stories. Graphics are added in the editing stage.

Switched with Graphics

This is a variant of switched taping. Here graphics for the studio portion of the program are added live during the switching of the program. This means that even less work needs to be done in post-production, as now all that has to be assembled in the master reel is the studio segments together with the stories. As soon as that is done the program is ready for broadcast or distribution.

Program to Tape

This option raises the bar considerably and requires a full studio, complete with cameras, control room, switcher and audio mixing console. Here the entire program is recorded live to tape. The graphical open is inserted from tape or disk into the program, the anchors read their story introductions live, and the pre-taped or edited segments are fed live into the program through the switcher. Graphics are also inserted live as needed in the studio. The final output is recorded to tape or disk live while it's happening.

While this option requires considerable resources in equipment, manpower, skill, and coordination, it produces a finished product without any further work. Recording the program to tape still allows for the option of fixing and flubs or making minor corrections or adding more graphics after the studio taping. The finished program can be broadcast or distributed however you want.

Program to Air

This is similar to the program-to-tape option except that the live production is transmitted directly to a live broadcast, either on closed circuit television, a public-access cable channel, or over the airwaves. What happens in the studio is live and happens only once; there is no opportunity for correcting what's been broadcast. No taping of the program is necessary, though it's always a good idea to do that for archiving, critiquing, and for re-broadcast or distribution in other forms such as tape, disc, or online.

Distribution

As many ways as there are to produce a finished program, there are at least as many to distribute a program. If the whole program is done live and broadcasted over the air or on cable, the production is over. Even if the program is live it can still be distributed in a variety of different ways. You don't have to limit yourself to only one means of distribution. There many avenues open to distributing and sharing video material. You can use any or all of them at different times.

One common way of distributing school programs is over a closed-circuit system that feeds the signal throughout the school or even through a whole school district. At an agreed time, often at the start of a particular class period, the program is fed through the closed-circuit system for everyone in all classes and offices that are connected.

A school or college video program is often distributed on a local public-access channel. These channels will often repeat a show, retransmitting it a number of times, which allows for access to a wider audience. Sometimes this is done live to air from your studio, but more often it is transmitted from a pre-recorded tape. This is an excellent means of having your shows seen by a large audience, which can help maintain the program, encourage participation, and give it legitimacy. It offers a venue for the larger school community to air issues and promote the spirit and achievement of your educational institution in academics, arts, sports, and other endeavors.

Another way to distribute your shows is on VHS tape or on DVD. By distributing the programs to classroom and through libraries to the larger community, your shows can be seen by a wide audience when it's convenient for them.

Another means of distribution is over the Internet. Compressing your program for streaming webcasts can be done either as a live broadcast or as a progressive download. Because of limitations of bandwidth it may be easier to break a program up into segments and mount them separately on linked web pages. The possibilities are numerous and expanding constantly as multiple types of information technology improve and become more efficient and more widely spread.

Studio Operations

News, sports, and special-events programming are perhaps the only programming left that is broadcast live. Morning entertainment programs like *Good Morning America* and *Today* are done live. Most late-night shows like *Late Night with David Letterman*, though they give the appearance of live broadcasts, are recorded earlier in the day. What these programs share in common is that they are centered on an anchor set, usually equipped with a desk behind which the anchors sit.

There are many ways to set up a studio, just as there are many uses to which a studio can be put. Usually what dictates what you can do is the space available and the budget you have. More of both and you'll be able to do more.

A simple presentation studio with one camera and an anchor can be created in a small space. No more than a small room or large closet is needed. For two or more anchors or for larger productions with multiple cameras and scenery, a large space is needed, especially for the lighting setup. A space as small as 10×20 feet can be used with more than one camera, but a larger space would be better. A number of schools use theatrical stages, as these afford good space and often have facilities for lighting already in place.

Figure 14.1 shows a typical studio arrangement used on a two-anchor set. Two of the cameras shoot across each other to the opposite anchor, while the third provides a wide shot. Cross-shooting allows for easier interaction between the anchors with less body movement. If the single cameras looked directly ahead to the anchors, the wide shot would appear unnatural, as if the two people were in a huff and not talking to each other.

It's traditional to number the cameras from left to right, so the camera on the left of the studio is Camera One. This numbering is used by the director in the control booth to identify and speak to the cameras. However friendly you are with your crew, get in the habit of using camera numbers as designations rather than the name of the camera operator. If someone changes position with someone, suddenly you'll have the wrong camera zooming in or out.

While the camera positions and operation are controlled by the director, usually by communicating over headsets, instructions are also passed to those in the studio through the floor manager. The floor manager tells the anchors, usually through signs and gestures, the timing of the program, counting down to the start, then directing them to which camera they should address. He or she also conveys through gestures when to slow down the delivery, when to speed up, and when to wind up the show.

Traditionally the anchors sit behind a desk, which doesn't have to be large, simply big enough accommodate people sitting comfortably side by side. The desk should be equipped with a modesty board so the camera cannot see the anchors' legs underneath the desk. The best place for the desk is about halfway between the farthest walls in the room. Moving the desk away from the background allows for easier backlighting and better separation between the subjects and the background. Don't move the desk so far from the background wall as to impede the movement of the cameras. They need to be far enough away from the subjects so that the shots can be framed without using too wide-angle a lens, which would distort the image. The cameras should be at least 10 feet away from the anchor desk, positioned at or slightly below the eyelines of the anchors. If the subjects are of different heights it's better to be slightly too low for one person than to be right for one and too high for the other. If the height difference is too great it may be necessary to use a stiff pillow or blocking under the chair of the shorter subject to adjust the difference.

The background should be plain and neutral in color. Avoid light, bright backgrounds or vivid colors, even if they're the school's colors. It's better to use a neutral background that can be lit with colored gels to add splashes of color to the image. It's also better to use graphical elements inserted over the picture to add color and interest to the image. This will allow you to create more variety and make the set more adaptable to a variety of purposes. The background is often draped to add texture to the scene, so the background is not a plain flat surface. Other textured fabric or carpeting can be used. Be careful though of textures that produce

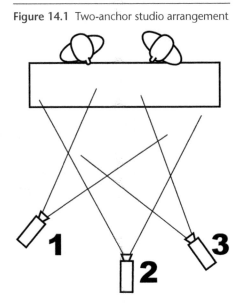

Figure 14.1 Two-anchor studio arrangement

patterns that may be reproduced on camera as moiré. This is a shimmering of color that you'll see on woven fabrics or tight patterns like herringbone tweed. The advantage of these materials though is that they can act as sound dampeners, absorbing reflective sound and making the room seem less hollow-sounding, which is often a problem in a large, boxy room.

If the studio space is large enough, another option that works well is to use the studio as your newsroom. Usually the background area of the studio is used for desks and other equipment. During the taping or broadcast of your program, the desks are usually populated. It's important that if this area is to be used as part of the set it be kept relatively neat, uncluttered and free of signs or objects that might distract the audience. It's also important that any activity in the background during taping be kept to a minimum. If you have the space and inclination to create this kind of set it can work very well and is used on many network broadcasts.

Lighting

Traditionally the lighting in an anchor studio is flat, soft, and flattering. This is especially important for aging anchors with lined faces and crow's feet, but for young people more modeled lighting can be used to produce a more pleasing image. Nonetheless, soft modeling work well. Lights like Photoflex boxes produce beautiful light without the harshness of direct spots. These can be used from almost directly in front of the subjects or from a slight angle to give better shaping in the image. Backlights can be focused spots, and should be used to separate the anchors from the background. Often the easiest way to do this is to securely mount a pipe near the ceiling a few feet behind the anchor desk. The backlights can be clamped to the pipe and double-fastened with a security chain. This can be done only if the ceiling is high enough to accommodate the lights without creating a fire hazard by having a hot lamp too close to ceiling surfaces, especially fiber tiles that can be scorched. The lights should be at least two feet away from the ceiling. If they hang down too low and cannot be aimed downward at sharp enough of an angle to avoid shining into the cameras, they should not be used.

Sound

Studio sound for anchors should be done through lavalier mics fed into a mixer. Some studios use lavalier wireless mics, but hard-wiring the mics to the mixer is generally safer and also means not going through a great many batteries. Lavaliers eliminate the poor acoustics of many studios. Acoustical dampening on the walls and ceiling will also help. Though it's not usually a danger, you should avoid making your studio so dead that it is completely reverberation-free. An acoustically dead space may sound just as awkward as an echoey space. If this is a problem, keep one wall bare with a hard, reflective surface to add a little life to the room, making it more like a living room than a soundproof chamber. A totally soundproofed room is not necessary, but as much separation from background sounds outside the studio is helpful. Outside, unexplained sounds can be distracting for the audience.

Sound for different types of productions should be handled with mics mounted on booms that can be aimed at the sound source. Usually two or three mics will cover the area of the average studio. Be careful that the audio signals from different mics do not cancel each other because the sound arrives to them at different rates. Monitoring the sound carefully on good speakers or good headphones will let you check for this. If there is a canceling effect, move one or both of the microphones so that they're in a different position. A small change in position will usually knock out the mic-canceling effects.

The sound mixer, video switcher, director, and technical director should be in a separate, soundproofed room that doesn't interfere with the studio itself. Usually the signals from the cameras are fed through small monitors that let those in the control room see what each of the cameras is doing at any time. In addition to the camera monitors the control room should have a main transmission monitor, which displays the output of the video mixer. This shows whatever is being transmitted or recorded. Next to the main program monitor is usually a preset monitor. The preset monitor shows what's on the second bus of the video mixer, what the mixer is about to switch to. In this way the director can always sees what's on air and on the camera he or she is about to cut to. Usually the preset monitor is right beside the program monitor.

Camera Setup

In addition to the video monitors in the studio it's a good idea to have a hardware waveform monitor and vectorscope attached to the preset monitor, which allows the technical director to make sure the video levels are correct on the cameras. This is useful before the shoot begins to make sure that all the cameras are correctly adjusted and using comparable white-balance and iris settings. Because different camera manufacturers' equipment behaves differently, it's best to use cameras of the same manufacturer and model. Otherwise color variations, edge detailing, and other discrepancies will be difficult to correct.

Before any studio session make sure to set up your production monitor properly. This is where it is so important to have hardware scopes, so you can calibrate your monitor and your video in the control room.

Monitors are calibrated with color bars. These can be generated by a small generator box like those from Horita. Most video switchers will also act as color bar generators. Monitors are set up using *pluge* (pronounced plooj, not plug), which stands for picture line up generator. Pluge is the array of black squares on the bottom right of the color bars. They help you calibrate your monitor to the correct NTSC black level specification of 7.5IRE. In the black swatch along the bottom, there are a set of three slightly different values of black. The bar farthest to right of the three should be slightly lighter than the others, set to 11.5 units. The two black areas to the left should be indistinguishable.

1. Turn up the brightness on your monitor until you can tell them apart. The bar in the middle should be correct NTSC black, while the one to the left is set to zero black.

Figure 14.2 Vectorscope and waveform monitors

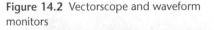

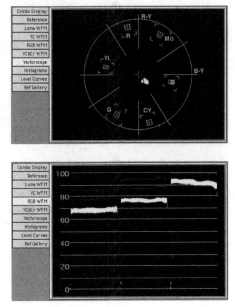

2. Turn the brightness back down just until you can't see the separation between the zero block and the 7.5. That's the point you're shooting for.

3. Next set the white level to 75 on your waveform monitor, using the white bar on the left side of the color bars. The bright white square in the bottom portion of the screen should reach 100. You may have to retweak the black settings.

4. Next set the color. Adjust the chroma so the bars shoot out to the targets on the vectorscope.

5. Finally, set the phase dial so that the bars fall onto the right color targets on the vectorscope. If one or more of the bars is outside the tolerance range by a significant amount, it might be time for a new monitor or at least to get it serviced by a technician.

Once your monitors are set it's time to set up your cameras. To do this use a chip chart (Figure 14.3) to set the white balance and exposure with a chip. This lets you see if the exposures match on the cameras and if there is any color shading affecting the image. There should be no color showing on the vectorscope when the grayscale chip chart fills the screen.

Set your white balance correctly and make sure your camera is on manual and not on auto white balance. Also make sure the camera exposure is set to manual and not to auto exposure.

The output of the video switcher (through the main program monitor) and the output from the audio mixing console are either fed to transmission or recorded

Figure 14.3 Chip chart

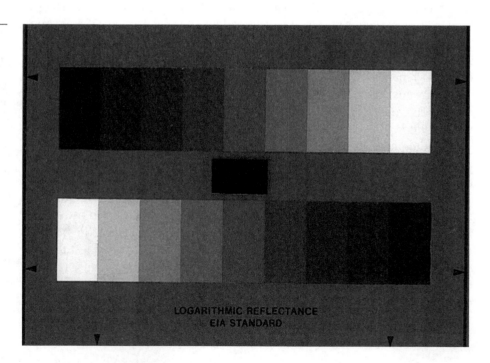

on tape for future distribution. Whenever a switcher is being used, communication between the director and the studio floor is essential. Ideally all the camera operators and the floor manager should be on headsets that can hear the control room. The headsets can either be hard-wired to a distribution box or connected wirelessly. Though it's helpful if those on the studio floor be able to talk back to the control room, it's not essential. The camera operators can communicate through signals using camera movement if necessary to indicate affirmative and negative, nodding the camera up and down being yes, and moving it from side to side being no. Moving the camera round and round in a circle usually indicates that the camera operator has a problem with the camera, though if it's an image problem this is usually seen immediately on the monitors in the control room. It's normal for the only voice on the communications system to be that of the director and occasionally the floor manager. Too much voice traffic on the system should be avoided as it can lead to confusion.

If no control room is available, it's best to record the scene with multiple cameras and to record each camera in isolation. The scene can then be edited on your computer. A program that supports multicamera editing will greatly facilitate this. Most systems can do this to some degree even if there is no multicam module.

Graphics and Special Effects

Graphics can be used to enhance a program and can be added either in the studio or in post-production when the final program is being assembled. If you are transmitting live to broadcast, your graphical elements and lower-third identifiers will have to be added live. This is done with a graphics generator attached to the video mixer. The graphics generator provides the text and other elements that can be overlaid on top of the video signal from the studio. Whoever operates the graphics generator should be able to monitor their work before it's fed to the video mixer to make sure the graphics are correct, look right, and that the text is spelled correctly.

Graphics generators can be used to add important information to a program as well as provide visual elements that are interesting. Graphics can include items such as sports scores, bar graphs, location and weather maps, and other visual displays. Most of these elements are prepared ahead of time in software applications like Adobe Photoshop or in animation applications like Motion or After Effects. More complex animations can be created using 3D applications such as 3DS Max or Cinema 4D. These elements are added to the program, from the graphics generator, from tape playback, or direct from disk. They can be switched live into a program through the video control room, or they can be added in post-production.

Graphics are important to any broadcast. See the section in Chapter 3 on Adding Titles for some suggestions on creating suitable titles over video. It's helpful to use a black or colored semi-transparent matte behind text to make it more legible over the picture.

Keying

Many studio productions are enhanced by using special effects such as chroma keying. By placing a subject in front of a green or blue screen, hardware or software can be used to key out the color background and replace it with another image. These of course work well only when there is no other green or blue in the image. So on St. Patrick's Day you may need to use a bluescreen.

The key to keying is to shoot it well. Poorly shot material just will not key properly. For chroma keying, the background bluescreen or greenscreen must be evenly lit and correctly exposed so that the color is as pure as possible. If there are shadow areas on the color screen these will be hard to key out. To avoid shadows make sure there is enough space separating the subject from the screen. Leave enough room so that any shadows fall on the floor and not on the screen. One way to light a background screen evenly is to shoot the scene outdoors. Sun or skylight is even across the range of the screen, and as long as there are no shadows falling on it, it should key easily if properly exposed.

Light the subject carefully so that the light does not brighten the background screen, creating hot spots on it. If you're using a greenscreen, it's helpful to use a pale pink or pale magenta gel covering the backlight. There will inevitably be some reflected spill light coming off the screen onto the subject's body from behind, most noticeably around the shoulders. This spill light can be suppressed by using the colored gel to counteract it. If you're using a bluescreen rather than the pale magenta gel, use a pale orange gel on the backlight.

Video, of course, and DV especially, has many limitations of color depth and saturation that make good keying difficult. Because of the way the format works, DV keys green easier than it does blue.

Another option for keying is to use a luma keyer. This keys out luminance values, either lighter or darker. Luma keying works properly only if you have a pure luminance value like pure white or pure black. Black is very hard to key well because almost inevitably there will be some darker, shadow areas in the image that will get keyed out inadvertently. Luma keying white is often easier, assuming there are no areas of bright clothing. Shooting against a white background and slightly overexposing the background so it washes out will allow for the area to be removed either with the hardware keyer in a video switcher or in software during post-production.

Live Operations

Schools are full of events that are great opportunities for trying out live studio operations on location. Sports events, performances, assemblies, all can be covered either live or live to tape with switched cameras and a director. The situation is the same as working in the studio except for the need to transport the equipment and the time needed to set everything up on location and tear it down again when you're done. It's a good idea to test all the equipment and rehearse the whole procedure in a studio before taking everything onto the location.

As in every studio situation, the key is good communication, the ability of the director to speak to the camera operators and control room technicians. If a good communications system can be put in place then the studio can be recreated anywhere, given enough time and enough cabling.

One of the principal issues with many remote setups is the length of cable runs needed to support good camera positions. On a football field you might want two or four grandstand cameras, two cameras on the sidelines, and two more in the end zones. This would give you ample but simple coverage for a game. Obviously it could be done with fewer cameras, perhaps as few as three, but eight would be a good number. This would require hundreds of feet of cabling to be laid out and secured. The video signal cannot travel long distances without deteriorating and will need amplifiers along the way. All this can take many hours to put into place.

During the production the director needs to be in complete control and ready for any eventuality. This can take a good deal of skill, practice and experience. Once everything is set up it can be tremendously exciting to create the program, responding to the ever-changing situation. It requires great concentration on the part of everyone involved—the director, the camera operators, the sound mixer, and especially the technical director. You cannot let your focus stray for a moment from what your doing and from the event in front of you. It's imperative that you be completely aware of everything that's happening on the field, court, stage, or auditorium so that you are getting the right shot and switching to right shot and hearing the right sound at any given moment.

You will constantly have to be trying to predict what will happen next and where the coverage needs to be before it even happens. Always have in the back of your mind where you will go when something goes wrong, when a camera fails, or when the play suddenly switches to somewhere unexpected. This is less of a problem for staged events like a play, which are usually well rehearsed, but for sports it's a frenetic effort to be constantly on point with the right shot at the right moment.

Live broadcasts of this type are great for all schools. They foster school spirit, serve to create a sense of community for those connected with the school, and provide an opportunity for responsible, productive, task-oriented collaboration between students. Live broadcasts also serve as an excellent venue for showing off a school district and its capabilities in the best possible light. It's great for public relations with the community, showing the educational system's accomplishments in a positive way.

This is your final project, and it gives you an opportunity to express yourself and create a piece of work that shows off your skills and your craft. The project should be no longer than 10 minutes and no less than three minutes. If the planned production is a live event or includes a live to tape event, the project can be longer. This project will be a major portion of your course evaluation. The content is for you to decide within the bounds of taste, appropriateness and copyright clearance.

Project: Final Project

1 Divide yourselves into groups of students who you want to work with. No group should be smaller than four or larger than seven, unless there are special production reasons.

2 Brainstorm your project proposal and prepare a detailed concept. This will have to be approved by the instructor.

3 Write a full script for the production in either two-column format or cinema format. If the project warrants or is a live event, a detailed storyboard and camera placement chart will have to be created. Once these materials have been approved by the instructor, production can begin.

4 The production should be shot with as much care and skill as possible.

5 Edit your project, adding titles and effects as needed.

Once all the projects are completed they will be viewed by the whole class, critiqued, and evaluated. The projects can be reworked or revised to some extent. Hopefully all the projects will be of a caliber that's suitable for broadcast and will be distributed and seen by as wide an audience as possible.

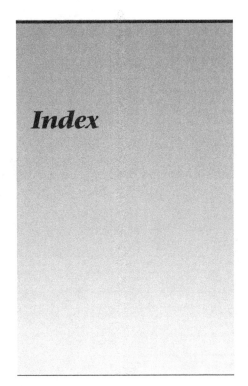

Index

Digital
Media
Academy

The Digital Media Academy is a premier technology training company offering a variety of courses in topics including web design, video production, 3D, digital media for the classroom, motion graphics, and game design. Courses are open to educators, teens, and adult learners. DMA instructors include nationally recognized technology experts and award-winning teachers. All DMA courses are offered for optional Stanford University Continuing Studies credit.

DMA is best known for its summer programs at prestigious locations like Stanford University. Each summer, hundreds of teens and adults attend one or more five-day immersion courses. DMA summer programs feature optional on-campus housing and dining and state-of-the-art facilities, all in a relaxed, collaborative environment.

DMA also provides on-site training to educational institutions and companies through its DMA on the Road program. Courses are customizable and available in any length from one to five days or more.

For more information about DMA and to register, call (toll-free) 866-656-3342, email info@digitalmediaacademy.org, or visit our website at www.digitalmediaacademy.org.